Paper

Marshall Cavendish London & New York

Edited by Linda Doeser

Published by Marshall Cavendish
Books Limited
58 Old Compton Street
London W1V 5PA

This material was first published by
Marshall Cavendish Limited
in the publication *Encyclopedia of Crafts*

First printing 1978

Printed in Great Britain

ISBN 0 85685 313 5

*Above: Crackers are not difficult
to make and can be enjoyed all the
year round. Surface decoration can
be chosen to suit any occasion.*

Introduction

Although paper has become a necessary and familiar part of our everyday lives, it is also an exciting and versatile craft medium. And now, with an ever-widening range of colours and textures becoming available, a revival of many of the traditional papercrafts, such as découpage, is taking place.

Paper teaches all the techniques of these and other fascinating crafts, including collage and quilling, illustrating the carefully explained step-by-step instructions and clear diagrams with beautiful colour photographs. Many of the projects require only simple and inexpensive equipment – decorative boxes for example can be made with household items. And once the basic skills have been mastered there are lots of suggestions for more advanced projects. These crafts are ideal ways of creating personalized gifts. Friends or relatives will be delighted to receive stencilled headed notepaper or a bound set of their favourite magazines – and children especially will love the clown crackers or the origami penguins. You can also learn to wrap your presents decoratively and make your own greeting cards as a delightful finishing touch.

Paper also suggests unusual ways to brighten up your home with highly individual items – a candle holder or vase of paper roses for example – or you may decide to create a collage and frame it. Whichever project you choose first, *Paper* will inspire you to try them all and fill your leisure hours with rewarding crafts.

Contents

Greetings cards

Slide across

Simple pop~up cards

Bright, original pop-up cards are easy to make and can be elaborated upon once you get the knack of a few basic techniques. The cards work·on the principle of a cut made across a fold in the paper. This frees a section of the paper which is then folded to give a three-dimensional pop-up that opens and closes to look like a winking eye, a talking mouth, or a quacking beak. The basic construction is simply the slit and the fold, but a wide variety of effects can be achieved by adding to this simple technique.

Above: A frog card with a winking eye and moving butterfly shape. It is a more sophisticated development of the technique described in this section.

Choosing the materials

It is important to select the right paper to work with. Paper that is too thin and floppy will not fold or stand satisfactorily, whereas thin cardboard is difficult to manipulate, and if it is coated the surface may crack. To begin with, use a good quality uncoated paper such as cover paper [construction paper], available in a wide variety of colours from art shops.

The slit principle

The simplest pop-up construction is made by cutting a single horizontal slit across a vertical fold in a piece of paper. This makes a basic opening inside which an eye, a message or a motif can be centred. Alternatively it can form a beak or mouth as illustrated in the completed frog and fish cards.

It is a good idea to experiment with lined paper to begin with, so that the creases can be made accurately. Fold the paper in half twice to make the card shape (fig. 1). Open up the card and fold the inside crease in the opposite direction. Snip horizontally through the crease not more than half-way across (fig. 2). Fold back the edges of the slit to make two right-angled triangles (fig. 3). Turn the paper over and fold these triangles over the other way (fig. 4). Repeat once or twice more to make the fold workable.

Open up the card flat (fig. 5). With the left thumb holding down the top crease, use the right forefinger to lift the pop-up (fig. 6). Press pop-up crease firmly (fig. 7). Repeat with the other half of the pop-up. Carefully shut the card, if necessary helping the pop-up outwards, and keeping the top and bottom creases folding with the centre fold of the card. Press the closed card flat firmly with the knuckles. Open and shut the card several times until it suggests a picture idea. If it reminds you of a duck you could add the face to match and write 'quack' inside the beak. If it looks like a baby bird, how about adding a worm dangling from the beak?

Decorating the cards

Use a variety of coloured stick-ons, gummed paper or paints to finish the design on your card. For example, trace off body shapes, plants and flowers from illustrations, cut out in coloured paper and stick them to the card. Experiment to find the different effects you can achieve by applying various finishes to the same basic pop-up like the cards illustrated overleaf. You can spend many enjoyable hours designing the decorations on your greetings card to suit the recipient, or a particular occasion.

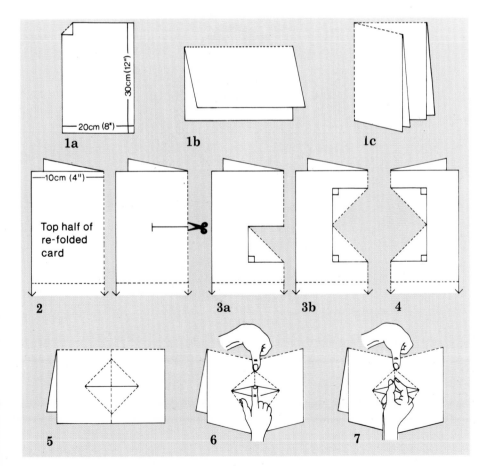

1a, b, c. Fold the paper.
2. Refold the card and snip·
through the crease.
3a, b. Fold back the edges of the
slit.
4. Fold the triangles over the
other way.
5. Open up the card flat.
6. Lift the pop-up.
7. Press the pop-up crease firmly.

The bird card

The brightly coloured robin card is based on the simplest pop-up construction described on page 6. Yellow paper has been used for the card, but you could use white instead and design a wintry scene to complete it.

Fold the yellow paper and make a 6.5cm (2½in) wide slit. Draw the body shape in black paper, using small coins for the outline of the wings, and then cut it out. Trace off and cut out the diamond beak shape from the black body. Stick the body on to the card so that the diamond cut out lies exactly over the pop-up shape. Cut out the red shape from gummed paper and stick in place.

Next, stick on file paper reinforcements for the eyes with inked pupils in the centre, or cut circles out of heavy cardboard or manilla. Complete the card by sticking on feet and legs cut from orange gummed paper, or draw them in orange crayon.

The bird card

You will need:
Yellow paper measuring 19cm by 30cm (8in by 12in).
Black paper measuring 19cm by 15cm (9in by 6in).
Scraps of red and orange gummed paper, or orange crayons.
File paper reinforcements or circles cut from manilla.
Scissors, glue.

Right: A cheerful robin card based on the simplest pop-up construction, which lends itself particularly well to the gaping beak shape.

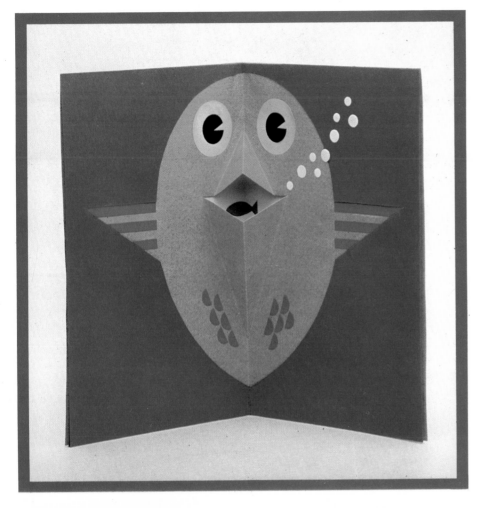

The fish card

You will need:
Blue paper measuring 19cm by 30cm (8in by 12in).
Green paper measuring 15cm (6in) square.
Scraps of dark green, white, yellow and black gummed paper, or crayons in the same colours.
Scissors, glue.

Left: The fish card with the pop-up shaped like a mouth.

8. Fold back the triangles to vary the mouth shape.
9. A small upper lip is formed by making the upper triangle smaller.
10. Use side plates to draw the big fish.
11. The trace pattern for the tiny fish inside the mouth.

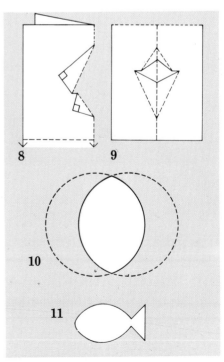

The fish card

Fold the blue paper and make a 5cm (2in) wide slit. The mouth shape is varied here as the top and bottom 'lip' are different sizes. This is simply done by folding back the triangles to different depths (fig. 8). If the upper triangle is smaller, this gives a small upper lip and a deeper lower lip (fig. 9).

Draw the large fish shape (fig. 10) and cut out from the green paper. Make a slit for the mouth. Stick the fish on to the card. Finish off with fins and scales in the dark green paper, a group of white bubbles and circular yellow eyes. Make the pupils from circles of black paper with a triangle snipped out.

Inside the pop-up, stick a square of white paper to the back of the card to look like a throat.

Trace off the tiny fish (fig. 11) and cut from green paper. Stick in place carefully in the centre of the mouth with a dab of glue.

9

Pop~up cards: fan folds

The pop-up principle already demonstrated can be developed to create all sorts of effects. The pop-up cards shown are based on a triangle folded from the centre crease of the card. The rocket trail is a simple pop-up traingle; the reindeer and the peacock combine the triangular pop-up shape with a cut inner edge.

The pop-up triangle

Fold the paper in half twice to make the card shape, then open up the card and refold it in the vertical crease. Fold down one corner from half-way down the central crease to half-way along the upper edge (fig. 1). Press sharply. Fold the crease over the other way and repeat once or twice to make the crease workable. Refold the card and, with the thumb and forefinger of the left hand keeping the crease in position, use the fingers of the right hand to ease the triangular pop-up shape into position (fig. 2). Carefully ease the card closed, then work it open and shut once or twice so the pop-up operates freely.

The instructions for making the cards show how to create effects with coloured gummed papers—but you may prefer just to draw the outlines, or to use crayons, paints or coloured inks.

Once you have tried these ideas, you will be able to think of many others – the reindeer can turn into a dog; the peacock's tail into a dress; the rocket trail into the rays of the Christmas star. It is not essential for the inside fold to be the same length as the outside one. The peacock's tail could just as well come half-way down the card, with the hedge stuck to or painted on the inside back of the card. But it is important to get the balance right or the card may topple forward. It is also advisable to work out new ideas on ordinary ruled paper before using more expensive, stiff paper.

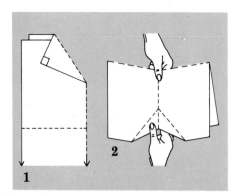

1. Make the preliminary folds of the rocket card.
2. Ease the triangular pop-up shape into position.

Above: The completed card. The trail is a simple pop-up triangle.

The rocket card

Take the blue paper, fold in half twice to make 10cm (4in) by 15cm (6in), and make the triangular pop-up shape described above. Cut out the cloud shape from the white gummed paper using a pair of compasses and a variety of radii to make arcs along one 20cm (8in) edge. Cut out the clouds. Fold the cloud shape in half to find the centre line, and fold a triangle from the centre crease to the same dimensions as the pop-out shape. Cut this triangle out of the cloud shape, and stick the cloud on exactly over the pop-up. Trace the triangle shape on to the yellow gummed paper and stick it over the pop-up.

Trace off the rocket shape (see over page), and cut it out of the silver gummed paper. Fold it in half to give the centre line, and stick the rocket on to the card so that the centre creases coincide. Use red and blue gummed circles for decoration.

The peacock card

Fold the dark blue paper in half twice to make 10cm (4in) by 15cm (6in). Using the compasses and a 10cm (4in) radius, draw an arc from the centre corner on the lower edge to the outer edge of the card (fig. 3). Mark the point where the pin of the compasses was placed. Take the small coin and place it half-way over the centre crease, against the arc. Move the coin along and draw a series of semi-circles, butting up against each other and the arc (fig. 4).

With the card folded along the vertical crease, cut out the tail shape through both thicknesses of paper (fig. 5). Make the triangular pop-up shape by folding sharply from the marked point to 2½ scallops from the centre edge (see fig. 6). Refold the card and ease the pop-up into position.

Cut a piece of green gummed paper 12cm by 20cm (5in by 8in) wide and stick it to the inside back of the card to form the background to the tail. Trace off the shape above the peacock's fan, cut it out of white gummed paper and stick it in position to form sky. Trace off the peacock's body from the shape given here, cut out of dark blue paper and stick in position.

Draw a line from the marked point where the pin of the compasses was placed to the edge of the second-to-last semi-circle on either

Above: The peacock card, which combines the triangular pop-up shape with a cut inner edge.

3. Draw an arc.
4. Draw a series of semi-circles with a coin.
5, 6. Cut out the tail shape and fold to form the pop-up shape.

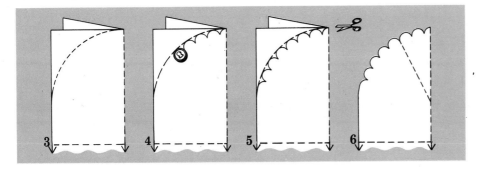

11

side. Then trace off the areas down to these lines and cut the hedge out of green paper, using the small coin again to give the scalloped edge. Stick in position. Decorate the peacock's tail with blue, brown and gold circles. Cut two semi-circles of white paper for the eye, inking a black pupil in the lower half.

The reindeer card

Fold the pink paper in half and cut a piece of green paper to the same size (this will form the inside background of the card). Fold the pink paper in half to make 10cm (4in) by 15cm (6in). Open up the card and refold it into the vertical crease. Draw or trace off the reindeer face shape given here and draw it on the edge of the pink card (fig.7). Cut out and fold the card back between the centre of the card and the point between the top of the nose and the antlers (fig.8). Work the crease back and forth a few times.

Draw the body shape on brown paper, making the reindeer's legs 4cm (1½in) apart. Cut the shape and stick the outline to the green card. Attach the pink card and reindeer head to the green background card, aligning the top of the two cards.

Cut out white circles from gummed paper for the eyes, with an inked dot in the centre for each pupil. Cut two half circles from yellow paper and stick in position on the bottom of the legs. Stick a red circle in place on the centre of the nose.

The reindeer card
You will need :
Pink paper 20cm by 30cm (8in by 12in). Green paper 10cm by 15cm (4in by 6in). Dark brown gummed paper 12cm by 20cm (5in by 8in). Scraps of red, blue and yellow gummed paper. Scissors, ruler, glue.

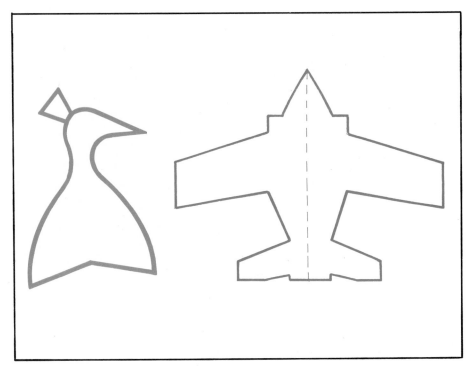

Right: The trace patterns for the aircraft and peacock.

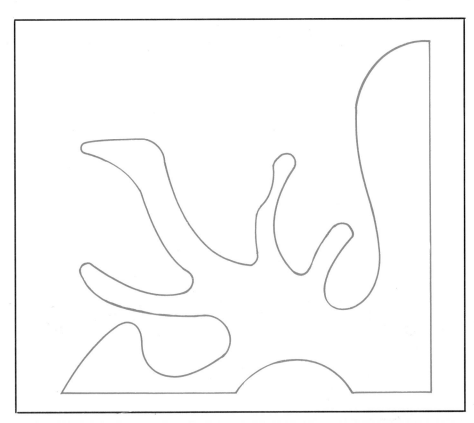

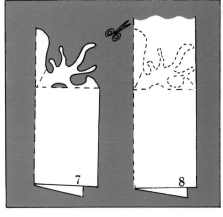

7. Trace the reindeer face shape.
8. Fold the card back.

*Left: The reindeer card,
with pop-up face and tusks.*

*Above left: The trace pattern for the
reindeer card.*

Pop~up cards with cut~outs

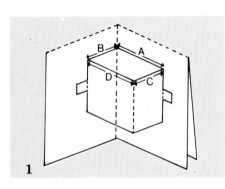

1. *The distance between the inside crease and vertical slit should be the same as the corresponding opposite side of the pop-up (ie.A=D and B=C).*

The jack-in-the-box card

You will need:
Dark brown paper, measuring 24cm by 52cm (9½in by 20in).
Magazine picture of jack-in-the-box, or similar, measuring about 22cm by 10cm (8½in by 4in).
Scissors, ruler.
Rubber-based glue.

To make the basic pop-up

Using the same paper as the main card, cut out two tabs and stick them to the sides of the pop-up, as near to half-way up as possible. If the tabs are placed too low, the pop-up will tilt forward, and if too high it will tilt backwards. The tabs should also hinge as near as possible to the widest points of the pop-up; if they are not hinged from the widest point they should extend past it. So positioning them correctly is a question of balancing these requirements. Fix the pop-up in position by slipping the tabs through two vertical slits cut in the card and taping or gluing them at the back. The position of the vertical slits can be determined by measuring the pop-up—the distance between the inside crease and the vertical slit should be the same as the corresponding opposite side of the pop-up (fig. 1 where A=D and B=C).

If the cut-out shape is from a magazine or newspaper and is rather flimsy, it may be necessary to glue it first to a piece of paper to give it body. The paper needs to be dark so that the print on the other side of the pop-up does not show through. Use rubber-based glue rather than a water paste as it will not smudge the type.

The jack-in-the-box

Fold the brown paper in half and in half again to make 26cm by 12cm (10in by 4¾in). Crease the pop-up shape sharply in half. Find a point half-way up the card and decide on the relation between this point and where the pop-up shape is widest. In the case of the card shown here, the central point on the left side of the card coincides with the widest point of the pop-up at the top edge of the box, so the pop-up hinge is flush with the edge of the pop-up itself.

On the right-hand side, the widest point of the pop-up is the tip of the fingers, so the tab extends to this width before being inserted into the slit (fig. 2). Cut two tabs from dark brown paper, 6cm (2½in) long and 2cm (¾in) wide. Glue or tape them to the back of the pop-up shape. Measure side C of the pop-up, from the centre crease to tab hinge. Mark a point on side B this distance

2. Make sure that the tab extends to the width of the fingers before being inserted into the slit.

Left: The completed jack-in-the-box card. The figure can be drawn freehand or cut from a magazine.

from the centre crease. Repeat with sides A and D, remembering in this case that the tab hinge is parallel with the widest point of the pop-up, the fingers. Open up the card and cut two vertical slits at these points, to the same depth as the width of the tabs. These slits can be cut with small, pointed scissors. Carefully slide the tabs through the slits, and glue or tape them to the card.

The heart card

Fold the lilac paper in half and in half again to make 17.5cm by 9cm (7in by 3½in). Keeping the solid circle at the centre, cut a rectangle 14cm by 15cm (5½in by 6in) from the doily. Spread glue over the centre circle and dot it over odd points on the paper lace, paying particular attention to the edges. Stick the doily

---

The heart card

You will need:
Lilac paper measuring 35cm by 18cm (14in by 7in).
Paper doily, with a solid centre 10cm (4in) in diameter.
10cm (4in) squares of red and brown gummed paper.
Cut-outs such as cupid, hands and flowers, all with tabs added to the sides.
Pair of compasses, scissors, ruler.
Rubber-based glue.

centrally inside the card as shown (fig. 3). Open out the card and, on the reverse of the side with the doily on it, mark a point on the crease line 4.5cm (1⅞in) up from the lower edge. With this point as the base and with the centre crease as the centre line, draw a heart 7.5cm (3in) deep (fig. 4).

Refold the card in half lengthways and cut around the top end of the heart through both thicknesses, to the point where the arc joins the tangent. Fold the heart over from this point to the base of the heart (figs 5a, b). Work crease back and forth several times. Refold the card, and ease the pop-up into position. Stick the square of brown gummed paper behind the heart on the inside of the card and cover the heart with red gummed paper. Fold the cupid shape in half vertically. Open up, and dab the side edges with glue. Lay the card flat and position the centre crease of the cupid over the centre crease of the card, inside the area covered by the heart but high enough for the cupid to be seen when the card is opened up. Stick down. Repeat this process with the cut-out joined hands and flowers shapes to complete the card.

3. Stick the doily centrally inside the card.

4. Draw a heart in the correct position.

5a, b. Fold the heart over from where the arc joins the tangent to the base of the heart.

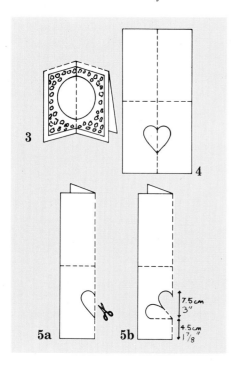

Right: The heart card, which would make an attractive and unusual Valentine.

Intriguing animated cards

Home-made cards are, of course, far more individual and personalized than the shop-bought variety—and therefore give greater pleasure. The making of them can also provide hours of fun: first thinking up ideas particularly suited to the recipient, then actually painting and cutting the design. By virtue of their movement, animated cards are particularly intriguing—both to design and to receive. In fact they are really lovely, amusing toys as well as cards, and liable to remain on the mantelpiece and to be enjoyed long after most other cards have been relegated to the wastepaper basket.

The basic principles

The cards illustrated here work on two different principles. The effect of the dog wagging his tail is achieved by means of a pivoted lever. The juggling clown is operated by a revolving disc. When the disc is spun the clown appears to juggle the coloured balls in the air. A simple background has been used for this card but you could create other circus scenes. A performing seal or a trapeze artist could be drawn in behind the clown instead of the audience. You do not need to be a great artist to make these types of cards. (You could always trace pictures from books or even use magazine cut-out figures if you don't feel up to drawing the images yourself.) But you do have to make careful calculations and accurate cuts to ensure that the animation works correctly, so it is worth studying and understanding the principles involved before trying your own designs. If you follow the detailed instructions given here, you will find that, although challenging, none of the cards is very difficult to make. And, once you have completed one or two cards, you will probably feel ready to adapt the principles to your own designs.

The dreaming dog card

Cut three pieces of cardboard each measuring 15cm by 10cm (6in by 4in) and mark them A, B and C with a soft pencil. Cut one piece of cardboard measuring 3cm by 10cm (1¼in by 4in) and

The dreaming dog card
You will need: Bristol board or similar thin cardboard measuring 50cm by 10cm (20in by 4in). Scalpel and pair of compasses. Ruler, soft pencil and rubber. Coloured felt-tipped pens, or paints. Small round yellow gummed paper shapes. A paper fastener or snap fastener and paper adhesive.

mark it with the letter D.

Place card A horizontally on the cutting table. Rule a 2.5cm (1in) square, using the bottom left-hand corner of the card to represent two sides of the square (fig. 1). Set your compasses at a radius of 2.5cm (1in). Place the compass point in the top right-hand corner of the square and draw a quarter of a circle into the left-hand

Pivot
Lever

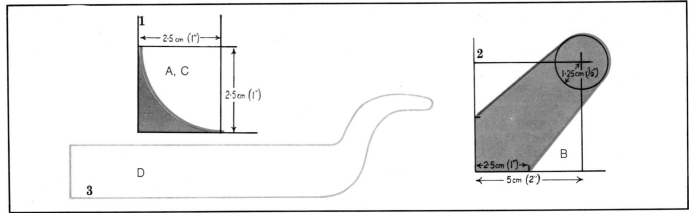

corner of the square (fig. 1). Place card C immediately under card A and cut along the semi-circular line to make rounded corners to both cards.

Rub out pencil calculations and trace the dog shape, but not its tail, on to card A. Line it up so that the base of the dog's feet is 1cm ($\frac{3}{8}$in) from the bottom edge of the card, and the tip of its nose is 1.7cm ($\frac{11}{16}$in) from the right-hand edge.

Colour and add yellow gummed shapes for extra interest. Cut a 1.5cm ($\frac{9}{16}$in) curved slit round the top of the dog's haunches—that is, where the tail protrudes in the photograph.

Place card B horizontally on the cutting table. Rule a 5cm (2in) square, using the bottom left-hand corner of the card as two sides of the square (fig. 2). Set the compasses at a radius of 1.25cm ($\frac{1}{2}$in) and, placing the compass point in the right-hand corner of the square, draw a circle (fig. 2). From the left-hand corner of the card measure 2.5cm (1in) up and also across.

From each of these points draw a line which touches the sides of the circle as shown. Join the two lines by curving round the upper arc of the circle, then cut out the whole area enclosed by the lines (fig. 2).

Trace the tail and lever (fig. 3) on to card D, colour and cut out. Carefully align and glue card B on top of card C. Place the tail and lever in position in the cut-out channel in card B, and fasten from the back with a paper fastener. Spread glue over card B and stick it to the reverse side of card A, being careful to align the cards carefully and remembering to slide the tail through the slit in card A before finally sticking down. By moving the lever up and down the dog will wag his tail.

The juggling clown card

Cut two pieces of cardboard each measuring 11.5cm by 18cm ($4\frac{1}{2}$in by 7in) and mark them A and B with a soft pencil. Cut one piece of cardboard measuring 13cm by 18cm (5in by 7in) and mark it with the letter C.

Take card A, place it vertically on the cutting table, and rule a line right down the centre of the card. Then rule a horizontal line across the card 7.5cm (3in) from the top (fig. 4). Place the compass point where the two lines cross, and draw a semi-circle with a radius of 4cm ($1\frac{1}{2}$in) above the horizontal line. Increase the radius to 5cm (2in) and draw another semi-circle. Round off the bottom of these lines just below the horizontal line and cut out the area enclosed by them (fig. 4). Also cut a very small hole, just large enough to take a paper fastener, at the point where the vertical and horizontal lines meet. Snap fasteners can be used as

Opposite: The dreaming dog card.

1. Make a rounded curve for the bottom left-hand corner.
2. The flare-shaped area, which must be cut out to allow for the movement of the pivot lever.
3. Lever and dog tail trace pattern.

The juggling clown
You will need: Bristol board or similar thin cardboard measuring 24.5cm by 36cm (10in by 15in). Scalpel and a pair of compasses. Ruler, soft pencil and rubber. Coloured felt-tipped pens, or paints. Round gummed paper shapes, in two sizes. Three paper fasteners or snap fasteners. Paper adhesive.

an alternative to paper fasteners.

Rub out the pencil lines and trace or draw the clown on to the card, cupping his hands round each end of the cut-out arc. Colour,

Revolving

Disc

Right: The completed clown card, shown here in its actual size so that it can be used as a trace pattern. When the disc is spun, this charming clown appears to juggle balls in the air. The disc is fixed with a paper fastener which doubles as a shirt button.

using gummed paper circles for faces of audience, eyes, nose, buttons and so on. Cut two small holes underneath the one already made in the clown's shirt. Place a paper fastener or snap in each of these two holes to represent buttons. Do not place the other (top) paper fastener or snap in position at this stage.

Place card C on the table in a vertical position. As before, rule one line down the centre of the card and a second across it 7.5cm (3in) from the top. Draw two more vertical lines on the card 7.5mm ($\frac{1}{4}$in) from the side edges (fig. 5). Place the compasses at the point where the horizontal and first vertical lines meet, and draw a circle that just touches the sides of the card. Open the compasses another 2mm ($\frac{1}{16}$in) and draw a second circle (fig. 5). Cut the card into three pieces and trim away waste as shown by the shaded areas in fig. 5. Cut a small hole in the centre of the disc, just large enough for the fastener. Colour the disc the same shade as used for the background of the clown. Place the disc behind card A and attach with a paper fastener or snap using the prepared holes. The front of the fastener now becomes the clown's top shirt button.

Stick the round paper shapes through the cut-out arc on to the disc, spacing them at regular intervals and turning the disc until a full circle of juggling balls is made.

Glue parts two and three of card C on to card B, aligning them carefully at top and bottom. Then glue them on to the back of card A, taking care to see that no glue touches the disc. By spinning the disc the clown will now appear to be juggling the balls from one hand to the other.

Designing your own adaptations

There are of course literally hundreds of designs and pictures that can be animated by using one or other of these techniques. It is great fun thinking up your own ideas, and devising the mathematical calculations needed to make them most effective. Don't feel that the pivot lever principle is restricted to pictures of animals wagging their tails. It can be adapted for all sorts of movement. For example to make a figure raise a glass for a toast; to show a kitten cleaning itself with its paw; to show a soldier saluting, a football player kicking a ball, a policeman waving on traffic, or a couple shaking hands.

Equally, the revolving disc need not show identical images at every turn. For instance, it could show an aircraft sky writing a message of greeting that is gradually revealed as the disc is rotated; or a group of different figures—men, women and children—walking on the bridge over a railway tunnel.

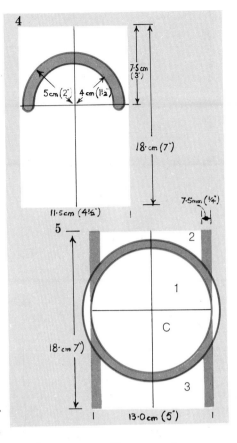

4. Cut-out arc allows revolving images on the disc to show through.
5. Measure and cut the disc.

21

Stencils

Cutting simple stencils

Stencilling has been successfully used to decorate everything from manuscripts and fabrics to walls and floors, more or less since the beginning of civilized history. The English term 'stencil' probably comes from the Old French *estanceler*—to cover with stars—because in early churches, walls and ceilings were often painted blue and then gold stars were stencilled all over them. The craft of stencilling was brought to a fine art in New England at the end of the eighteenth century and beginning of the nineteenth.

Stencils are a quick and easy way of reproducing patterns by hand and can be used to give an individual touch to most homes or to create original, personal greetings cards, letter headings or (using fabric dyes) to hand-print lengths of material for clothes. Stencilling isn't a difficult craft to learn, although it needs care and thought in the preparation stages.

Stencil paper

Thick stencil paper, specially treated to withstand repeated applications of paint, can be bought from art supply shops but there are cheaper alternatives. In eighteenth-century America, a great deal of decorative stencilling took the place of wallpaper and floor coverings. The craftsmen used leather stencils or, more often, heavy paper stiffened with oil and paint, with a bevelled edge to ensure a sharp outline. Modern stencillists can use heavy brown paper coated with lacquer, thick aluminium foil, or cardboard, rendered non-porous by the use of a commercial sealer, PVA glue or several coats of varnish. If you are only going to make one or two stencils, you can use thick, untreated cardboard, although this will not last for much longer than two impressions. You can also use thick acetate film. Because this is transparent, it can be placed over the pattern and cut without tracing first, which is a great time saver. Beginners are advised to use stencil paper or thick acetate film

Tools

Cutting tools   Depending on the material which you are using,

Above: With stencils it is easy to reproduce original designs on a variety of surfaces. Use a sharp knife or blade to achieve smooth edges.

Above and opposite: Stencilling is an easy craft, particularly suited to those who do not have the confidence to draw freehand designs. Stencil a stunning floral 'mat' on your floorboards.

you will need either a light scalpel [artist's knife] or a heavy-duty trimming knife. Both are available from craft shops and have removable, replaceable blades. These blades are all dangerously sharp and have to be used with great care. Always keep them away from children. The scalpel [artist's knife] has a thin, flexible, usually very pointed blade which is quite difficult to change and which should be stuck into a rubber [an eraser] when not being used. The heavy-duty trimming knife has a standard blade for general cutting but for cutting cardboard and paper you need a blade with a sharp edge that points downwards. You can buy a blade for lino [linoleum] cutting—an angled blade for slitting and trimming and a convex blade for scoring and cutting. One very good type of cutting tool has a long, multi-edged blade, the tip of which can be snapped off when it has become blunt.

Metal ruler Another tool needed is a metal ruler for cutting straight lines—a wooden edge soon becomes chipped and therefore inaccurate, and you should in any case cut straight lines against a metal rule or the cutting tool may slide off and cut you.

Tracing paper to transfer designs on to the stencil paper.

A wooden board to cut on in order to avoid damaging the surface of your table.

Stencil brush This should be a round one with a flat-cut surface but not too big because, if it is, it will hold too much paint which will seep under the stencil edges. Clean brushes well after use.

To make a stencil

Before starting work, make sure the working surface is firm. Tape the cutting board to a table, then tape the stencil paper to the board. Then you can begin to cut.

When cutting any stencil, make sure that the outside edges of the stencil are square and even, as this will help with the spacing and placing if you want to repeat your pattern over a large area.

How to cut straight lines Place the metal ruler along the line you wish to cut. Hold the ruler firmly in place with one hand, keeping fingers well out of the path of the knife. Hold the knife in the other hand, either like a pencil or a table knife, whichever is the most comfortable. Keeping your arm rigid, draw the knife against the ruler without angling the blade but keeping it absolutely straight on the line, leaning down on the knife and drawing it backwards towards you. Don't try to cut right through all in one go but cut lightly at first, then more and more firmly until the line is cut through. It is usually easier to cut a long line a little at a time.

Cutting circles and curves Again, never angle the knife to the left or right but lean it backwards towards you. Hold the paper

1

2

3

firmly, keeping the fingers well away from the path of the blade. Untape the paper from the board, cut a little of the stencil at a time, then turn the paper and cut a little more until the circle or curve is complete.

Planning designs for stencils

Except on thin paper or on cardboard that is being used, perhaps, for one or two repeats, even the sharpest knife will have difficulty in cutting very intricate designs, so keep your stencil patterns simple to begin with. When cutting out a shape of any kind from a stencil, it must be attached to the outside border of the design or the cut shape will simply fall out.

There are two ways of attaching the shape. Either leave linking tags (or stays) attached to the outside border, or make the shape large enough to touch the frame at various points, which will hold it in place (fig. 1).

Stencils can either be negative—i.e. the background is cut away to form the design (fig. 2)—or positive, when the actual design is cut away (fig. 3). So from one design you can get two completely different-looking stencils. Stencil patterns can also be varied by colouring different areas in different colours, adding strong colour on top of pale colours at a later stage. It is also possible to cut two-part stencils that fit on top of each other, so that first one colour is printed and, when that is dry, another design in another colour is placed on top. When doing this, cut register marks (fig. 4) on both stencils so the designs will fit accurately over each other and give a clear image.

Once you have become adept at cutting out simple shapes you can progress to making more complex ones. Wallpaper patterns, floor and wall tiles or old books will provide design ideas.

4

 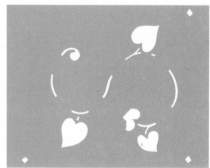

1. Design touching the frame
2. Result of negative stencil
3. Result of positive stencil
4. Two-part stencil with register marks.

Paper quilling

Introduction to the craft

The art of quilling, or decorating with rolled papers, is an ancient one. It has the appearance of great intricacy and complication but the actual process is, in fact, relatively simple. Thin strips of paper are wound tightly round a stick and then released. As the paper springs open the size and shape of the quill are determined by arresting the movement with adhesive and pinching into shape. The quills are then assembled into a pattern and stuck down on to the surface to be decorated. Another early name for quilling was paper filigree—and this accurately describes the original paper imitations of gold filigree used in ecclesiastical art as early as the fifteenth century. Religious decorations, medallions and pictures then incorporated beads, metal threads and shells, and gaps were filled with coils of tightly rolled paper. By the late eighteenth century quilling had become a fashionable craft for young ladies of leisure. They refined it to the flatter form we know today—that composed entirely of rolled paper. Typical of their style of design was the filling of a strip paper outline with as many tightly packed paper rolls as possible. They decorated anything from boxes to furniture panels.

There is certainly something very soothing and unhurried about the art of quilling. The gentle action of twirling and pinching the quills into shape can be enjoyed whenever you have an occasional quiet moment. And the prepared quills can be stored in boxes until you have time and inspiration to settle down to designing and arranging your composition. You can use your quills for small things such as greetings cards, to decorate gift boxes or crackers, to make pretty mobiles or jewelry. Or, on a larger scale, you can decorate lampshades or make pictures, fire-screens, mirror frames, trays or table tops. The possibilities are almost endless. You can use paper quills only or hark back to the origins of paper filigree and introduce richness and depth to your decorations by adding a few beads or stones here and there.

Paper and tools

Originally the strips of paper were rolled round a quill—hence the

Left: Strips of quilling paper, a cocktail stick or hair grip [Bobby pin], paper adhesive and scissors are all you need to make quills.

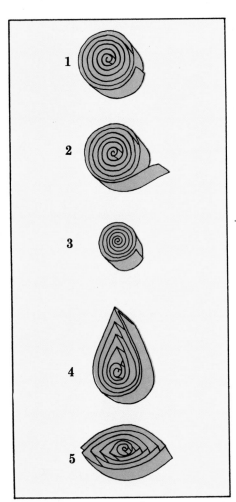

1. Loose coil
2. Loose open coil
3. Tight coil
4. Tear-drop
5. Eye shape

name of the craft. Nowadays this delicate-looking craft is usually done on a split cocktail stick or, easier still, a hair grip [Bobby pin] with the open ends cut off with tin snips or pliers so that the two sides are parallel and hold the paper firmly. You will also need some paper adhesive, a cocktail stick or matchstick for applying it, and, of course, quilling paper. Special quilling paper is available from some craft and hobby shops, but colours are usually somewhat restricted. Carnival streamers are just as suitable and often easier to buy. They come in packets of assorted pastel shades. You can use them singly or have fun combining two colours, either winding them simultaneously or using one after another in the same quill. If you choose the latter combination, join the end of one coloured strip to the beginning of the other before you start quilling. Just overlap the two strips of paper and secure with a spot of paper adhesive.

The basic method

The length of the paper strip and the number of rotations you make are up to you (one part of a multiple pattern, however, must of course be the same as the others) but for experimental purposes a 20cm (8in) strip is about right.

Loose coil is the most basic quilled shape and a good one to start practising first (fig. 1). Place one end of a 20cm (8in) strip of quilling paper or colourful carnival streamer in a prepared hair grip [Bobby pin]. Check that it lies level with the top of the grip. Then rotate the grip [pin] with one hand and roll the paper on to it with forefinger and thumb of the other hand. Roll the paper slowly to begin with so that it spirals quite tightly, and check that the top edge of the spiralling paper remains level. When the paper is completely rolled, give it a gentle squeeze with the fingertips to tighten the curve before releasing.

Hold the coil gently with one hand and remove the hair grip [Bobby pin] with the other. It may be necessary to unwind the paper a little to release the tension before you can remove the grip [pin]. Ease the coil to the size you wish. Then apply a little adhesive to the loose end of the paper strip and stick it on to the spiral of paper immediately inside so that the quill holds its shape firmly.

Loose open coil is made in exactly the same way but left to spring free without any sticking (fig. 2).

Tight coil is, as the name implies, not allowed to spring free but eased out or stuck on to itself before removing from the grip [pin] (fig. 3).

Tear-drop is made like the loose coil. After sticking, pinch one

30

side to a point, with the stuck end of the strip coming down to the point (fig. 4).

Eye shape is made like the tear-drop but both ends are pinched. It is particularly effective if you allow the centre of the spiral to remain intact, like a round pupil (fig. 5).

Leaf-shape is like the tear-drop but the whole is allowed to elongate, then pinched with gentle curves in opposite directions (fig. 6).

S-shape Roll one end of the strip to just over half-way. Then turn the strip and roll the other end. Roll it in the same direction, again rolling to just over half-way. Let it spring free. No adhesive is necessary (fig. 7).

Scroll is the same as the S-shape but with both coils on the same side of the strip. Again no adhesive is needed (fig. 8).

Heart is similar to the scroll but the strip is first creased in half (fig. 9).

V-shape is exactly the same as the heart but rolling away from the inside of the crease (fig. 10).

Decorating cards and boxes

It is sensible to start by decorating a small flat surface (such as a greetings card or small box), and to choose a simple design. The natural shapes of your quills will suggest subjects, but abstract designs can be equally effective—gain inspiration from the twirling shapes of wrought iron work. Simple designs like these, which involve a few quills only, will not require a pattern guide for sticking. Lay the quills on top of the surface to be decorated and arrange into a pleasing composition. Then remove, one by one, and stick into position.

Hold the quill in one hand and use a match or cocktail stick to spread a drop of paper adhesive across the bottom edge of the centre coils. (Sticking the central coils only, and leaving the outer ones free, is not only less messy from a technical point of view but it will also give your composition more sense of movement.) Lightly press the quill on to the surface to be decorated.

Filigree mobiles and jewelry

Conversely, when the designs are free-standing, adhesive is applied to the outside coil of each quill only along the curved side at the point of contact between one quill and its neighbours. In order to do this successfully, it is a good idea to make yourself a little work board.

To make a simple work board to use for quilling, take a piece of thin plastic foam, styrofoam or other soft but firm material and

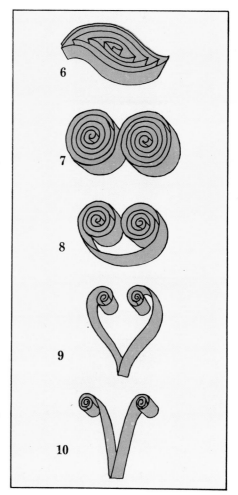

6. *Leaf shape.*
7. *S-Shape.*
8. *The scroll.*
9. *Heart shape.*
10. *The V-shape.*

lay it on a flat surface. Cover with a piece of transparent waxed paper or tracing paper, stitching or stapling it on to the foam at the corners to hold it firm. If your design is a complicated one, you can slip a pattern under the transparent paper so you have a design guide to follow when sticking.

Lay one quill on the transparent paper and place a pin through the central hole to prevent it from slipping. Take a second quill and spread a little adhesive along the outside coil at the point where it will touch the first quill. Abut and lightly press the two quills together. Then place a pin through the second quill to hold it in position. Making up the design as you go, or following your predetermined pattern, stick and pin the rest of the quills until the composition is completed. When the adhesive has thoroughly dried and the pins have been removed you will be able to lift your free-standing quilling away from the work board. Hang the quilling from a thread for a mobile. Varnish jewelry items with several coats of clear acrylic or polyurethane spray for strength and attach to suitable findings.

Above: It is quite easy to make your own jewelry with beads and paper quills.

Right: This delicate-looking butterfly involves many quills and takes some time to make but the result is a delightful mobile.

More advanced projects

Although papers other than carnival streamers and special quilling paper will require measuring and cutting into strips, the opportunity to use a wider choice of textures and colours is very inviting. Combination papers are unsuitable: the two layers tend to argue in the process of quilling, but almost any flat single paper (excluding crêpe) can be used successfully. The weight of the paper is immaterial providing it can be rolled—very heavy papers may require a dab of glue between coils to retain the spiral pattern.

Sheet acetate can be used and is an exciting material for this craft. If you find it difficult to glue acetate quills, secure them by stapling instead, but be careful to locate the staples so that they will not spoil the effect of the final design.

Gift ribbon, the decorative sort that sticks to itself when wet, is another quite different material that can be used for a variation of quilling.

Unlike conventional quilling, decorative ribbon is held in shape by sticking. Ring the ribbon round your forefinger, licking the end of the ribbon to secure the loop. Then make a second ring, a little larger than the first, sticking it to the inner ring at the same point as before. Add subsequent rings, increasing their size a little each turn and sticking as before.

Strips of woodshavings can sometimes be bought from hardware shops or craft shops. Once they have been soaked in water, these become pliable and can be used for quilling. Follow the method used for decorative ribbon, using a dab of glue to hold each coil to the next.

Ornate Victorian quilling

During the Victorian period, the art of quilling reached the heights of popularity—a pastime practised by every young lady of leisure, who favoured designs involving numerous loose coil quills tightly packed into areas outlined by strips of coloured paper. This taste for the intricate, combined with a certain snobbishness, led to the popularity of quilled shield decorations.

At that period the shields were usually framed and hung as pictures, mounted on to fire–screens or used to decorate furniture panels. But they could equally well be used to make decorative and unusual tray or table tops. Protect the paper design by setting in a recessed frame and cover with a sheet of glass or acrylic such as Perspex [Plexiglass].

Light reflections

Light shining through the spiral shapes of paper filigree creates interesting effects. Quilling decorations can look very handsome around a lampshade, for example, and a quilled border framing a mirror is even more exciting. The image is repeated in the glass of course and, if a' material such as Melinex [Mylar] is used for quilling, the reflection is shimmering. Silver Melinex [Mylar] is a filmy material with a glossy polished finish that reflects light well. It is pliable and can be cut with scissors. Melinex [Mylar] comes in rolls, usually about 48cm (19in) wide. It can be bought by the metre (yard) from most stationers and some art and craft shops. Different weights are available: medium-lightweight is usually best for quilling.

Silver Melinex [Mylar] mirror frame

Cut the Melinex [Mylar] into 100 strips 1cm ($\frac{1}{4}$in) wide across the width of the roll. Roll each strip round your forefinger five times, making a slightly larger coil at each turn. Staple the coils together at one point, leaving the remaining strip as a tail piece (fig. 1). Join the tail end of one quill to the centre of the next quill with a tiny spot of glue, placing the quills on alternate sides of the joining strip (fig. 2). The distance between each quill should be about 6cm ($2\frac{1}{2}$in). Join quills in groups of eight, then curve the joining strip into the pattern shown in fig. 3.

Repeat this process until all the quills have been used up. The last group will consist of four quills only, forming the first half of the pattern. Lay the quills round the mirror and, if necessary, adjust a curve here and there to ensure the quills make a well-shaped border frame. Then remove the quills, one group at a time, apply a little glue to the bottom edge of quills and joining strip and stick on to the mirror, pressing down lightly into position.

Free-standing 3D designs

Fairly heavy papers can be quilled to produce free-standing three-dimensional designs. Using heavy cover paper [construction paper], and strips of varying widths (widest at the bottom and tapering at the top) will help to stabilize the design.

Silver Melinex [Mylar] mirror frame
You will need: 1 mirror glass 76cm by 41cm (30in by 17in) with bevelled edges. 1 metre (39in) medium lightweight silver Melinex [Mylar]. Small stapler. Ruler. Scissors. Clear general purpose glue.

Opposite: Silver Melinex [Mylar] quills make a shimmering border for a sheet of mirror glass.

Quilled floral bouquet
Self-adhesive ribbon is ideal for making a pretty vase of quilled flowers. Use green ribbon for stalks and leaves, and colours of your choice for the flowers themselves. The choice of colours, sometimes two-toned or with gilt threads running through the

1. *Staple the coils together.*
2. *Join the quills.*
3. *Join the quills together in groups of eight.*

35

ribbon, and silky-looking finish make this material particularly attractive for fantasy flowers—to use as mobiles or arrange in vases.

Stalks are made of thin, pliable wire (such as florist's wire) round which green ribbon has been wrapped (moistened after each twist to make it self-adhesive). Bend the top of a stalk back on itself to make a small central circle—a base on which to glue the flower petals. Glue leaves directly along the length of a stalk as shown in the photograph. Cut a piece of styrofoam or floral foam to fit a small vase. Plant the base of each stalk in the foam, and arrange your everlasting bouquet.

Below: An everlasting quilled floral bouquet.

Collage

Creating a simple collage

The word 'collage' (derived from the French verb *coller* meaning to glue) describes the abstract art form of juxtaposing and gluing together different materials to create a picture. Of all picture-making techniques, collage is probably the most versatile—and therefore of universal appeal to adults and children alike. It is simple and great fun to do. Gluing requires no particular skill, and it is utterly absorbing to see the various effects that can be achieved by relating materials of differing texture, shape, colour and pattern. Compositions can be as straightforward or as intricate as you wish; they can be flat or three-dimensional, and you can use more or less whatever materials you care too choose —from used matchsticks to car tyres.

Paper collage is, of course, restricted to using paper materials only. This makes it more manageable than some other types of collage, and costs are negligible if you use papers to be found in the home—but don't be misled into thinking this means it is any the less enjoyable or creative. In fact, paper collage provides a particularly fascinating and challenging exercise because it is only when you start a serious search that you become aware of just how rich and varied is the choice of papers available. And it's only when you start combining them that you realize the almost infinite variety of effects that can be achieved.

Papers in the home

Just go into the kitchen, see how many different papers you can find there—and you may well come to the conclusion that there's no need to go out and buy special papers for making a collage. Probably you will find a thick brown paper shopping bag or, perhaps, a prettily decorated one; absorbent paper towels; semi-transparent grease-proof paper; gleaming cooking foil; labels in decorative shapes and colours in jam jars, cheese boxes, canned foods and soft drinks bottles; lacy paper doilies; cereal cartons and other packets in thin cardboard.

The living room will yield still more. Old picture postcards, perhaps with foreign stamps, thick writing paper and flimsy air mail paper (coloured, ruled or plain), envelopes of various shapes, sizes and colours, brown wrapping paper, perhaps some pretty wrapping papers, corrugated paper, blotting paper, shiny sweet [candy] and chocolate wrappers, garden seed packets, bus, train, theatre and old air tickets, an invitation card, cheque book stubs, receipts from cash registers, old photographs and negatives, leftover pieces of wallpaper, cigarette packets and gold backed cigarette packet lining paper, paper napkins, and, of course, magazines and newspapers.

Using colour, texture and shape

As you can see, the choice of papers is huge. And it is quite extraordinary how many and varied are the effects that can be achieved depending on the way papers are combined. Experiment with a square each of white cardboard, scarlet tissue and kitchen silver foil. See how many different combinations of texture, colour and pattern can be made with only these three papers. For example, a geometric pattern with the squares laid side by side and

Left: Choosing and cutting out suitable material from magazines is something to be enjoyed by all the family. It is a good idea to sort out and classify items as you come across them.

39

just overlapping will show each colour alone, their interaction and changes where they overlap. Accentuate the different textures by sprinkling the tissue with a little water and rubbing it with a cloth so that it has a delicate streaked sunset look, and fringe the foil like a gleaming flowing mane or waving grasses. Use the papers for three-dimensional movement, rolling the card like a log and wrapping it with superimposed layers of foil and tissue cut into flame shapes. Or cup the tissue into giant poppy shapes and scratch the foil to make veined leaves. The permutations are almost endless.

Right: A collage which uses numerous curved shapes and centres on a single cut out figure. Interest is added by optical illusions of texture—even the 'embroidery' is cut from magazine illustrations.

Collecting special papers

It is fun to collect papers with a particular project in mind. For instance, you might search out and put to one side papers of the same colour tone, seeing just how many different textures and patterns there are. You might choose a subject and search out as many different visual interpretations of it as you can find. Or, on holiday [vacation], you might collect postcards, a menu, your tickets, the label from a local wine, a theatre programme and a local newspaper to form the basis of a nostalgic memento collage. But there is no need to collect vast quantities of different papers before embarking on a project of this sort. Most collages are simply creations of the moment and should be enjoyed as such. The Christmas tree collage illustrated overleaf is made from sweet [candy] papers—and serves as an excellent example to prove that a little imagination can turn the simplest of materials into a delightful and very effective collage.

Below left: A collage which takes the apple as its subject and shows the fruit in many guises. Large apple shapes, cut from a coloured magazine, shiny red paper, cellophane and orange tissue are surrounded by smaller apples.

Below right: This holiday moment collage is called 'Birthday Breakfast in London'. The use of blue holds the composition together well and the pleated airmail letters add an element of interest.

To make a paper collage

Use rubber based adhesive for papers which are to be stuck flat, and the stronger, clear, general purpose glue for three-dimensional effects when only part of a piece of paper is to be glued on to the mount. Always spread glue in a thin even coat as this adheres more effectively and is less likely to mark papers than large blobs of glue. Tissue papers and magazine papers can be lightly ironed to make them crisp. Cellophane can also be ironed very gently if it is first placed between two sheets of paper—but cellophane is best abandoned if very badly crumpled as this light ironing will have very little effect. It is a good idea to start by laying a few pieces of paper on the table to form the basis of your composition. Make a quick sketch on rough paper and use this as a guide for gluing into position. As you get more skilled, and your feeling for contrasting and complementary textures, colours and designs develops, you will probably find it unnecessary to make this preliminary testing and can rely on your creative judgment to build and glue your collage immediately.

Below: An effective collage made from sweet [candy] papers, and a kite collage in which coloured negatives have been used.

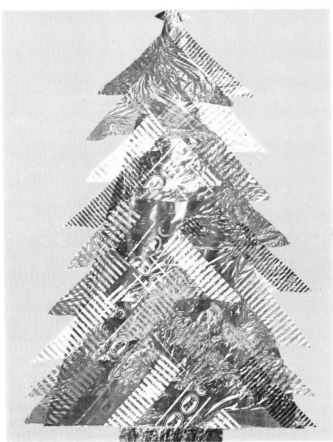

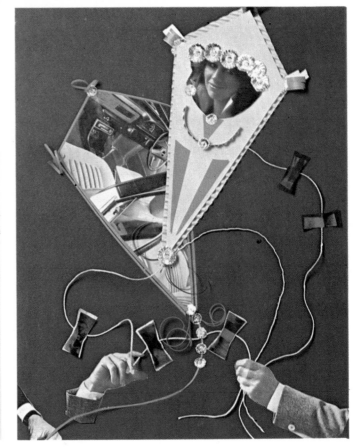

More collage materials

Other materials besides paper can be incorporated into a collage and worked into a design to give greater depth and atmosphere, or to highlight a certain aspect of the composition.

Basically, the methods are the same as earlier in this chapter. To make these collages, you will need the same materials and tools as before—plus, of course, additional materials of your choice and adhesives suitable for sticking them down firmly.

Unification by colour

An interesting collage can be made quite quickly and simply by putting together all sorts of objects and materials that are not necessarily closely related in subject matter, but are unified by a colour scheme. The three-dimensional 'Red and Silver' collage illustrated overleaf is a well executed example of this style.

As you can see, the oddments used in the collage are very diverse. They could have resulted, all too easily, in a messy composition that would prove tiring to the eye. But, because the designer has disciplined the work, the various oddments are clearly held together to form a very pleasing composition. The two main elements of restraint involved are careful use of colour and basic simplicity of line. Note how the background silver is picked up again and again throughout the design, first by the silver braid, then with the toy bike, the disc, necklace clasp and safety pins.

Equally the use of red is well balanced with some solid blocks of colour (shiny surfaced paper squares, bricks raided from the children's toy box, and the ballpoint pen), and other, lighter, more airy touches—the playing cards and the amusing sparkling teardrop shapes from a broken necklace.

Stark simplicity has been used to arrange the background shapes. Not only are the red paper shapes set firm and square, but the rest of the composition has been built up to echo their careful formality. Note the emphasis on upright vertical lines in positioning the crossword puzzle, the transparent plastic ruler, the king of diamonds and even the plastic letters. This gives a sense of order and provides an excellent foil for small areas of movement. In

Right: 'Red and Silver' collage in which the designer has co-ordinated a wide variety of objects into one cohesive composition. Repeated use of vertical lines for background shapes and restriction to two basic colours cleverly prevent the collage from becoming too 'busy'.

fact, it is precisely because of this restrained background that the directional arrangement of safety pins and the angled elephant card gain in impetus and so successfully lead the eye to the central focal point of the composition.

Using contrasts for impact

A very effective method of emphasizing the interest of a paper collage is to incorporate other materials, the textures of which contrast strongly with the paper—thus throwing each and every item into bold relief.

The three-dimensional collage 'Industrial Revolution' is a powerful example of this method. Papers, plastics and metals have been combined to produce an exciting marriage of strange contrasts, and the design is such that the collage has tremendous visual depth and atmosphere. The skyline factory chimneys have an

Below: 'Industrial Revolution' is a three-dimensional collage in which paper, metal, plastic and a strong sense of design combine to produce a composition of visual depth and atmosphere.

almost frighteningly explosive quality. But clever composition draws the eye through menacing belches of smoke, down the heavy, swinging, crane-like bars and hooks and ropes, into the comparative peace of the production line. Here rows of materials and repeated interlocking cog-shapes churn on with a sense of purpose and provide the collage with a reassuring sense of symmetry and rhythm.

The background sheet of paper is in fact white. Cut the orange sheet slightly wider than the background paper and cut to give silhouettes of factory roofs, chimneys and cooling towers. Hold orange against white and spray with black watercolour or watered down black ink (you can use an old tooth brush and a knife for spraying). Dip the brush in the liquid, then stroke the bristles with the knife—see illustration. Before the spray is dry a piece of damp cotton wool [absorbent cotton] is lightly swirled across certain areas to produce a smoky effect. The orange paper is then moved slightly to the left, trimmed to fit and glued down, leaving sharp white margins between black spray and orange buildings. The white smoke lines are drawn with adhesive squeezed direct from the tube on to the paper (this is done before ink spraying but remains white because it resists the ink). Add strands of steel wool later.

Other papers are heavily textured: sandpaper, corrugated paper and textured wallpaper, all cut in circular shapes of varying sizes. Metal and plastic objects raided from the tool box are cleverly combined and superimposed to give precise, machine-like detail. Note how the line of the crane is counter-balanced by the long masonry nail (the only two vertical lines in the whole composition), and the flowing row of small round objects at bottom left is balanced by groups of corrugated fasteners (bottom right) also forming a waving line.

Creating harmonious effects

The introduction of other materials need not necessarily result in a collage with such forceful impact as 'Industrial Revolution'. Very subtle effects can be achieved by using one type of paper only, showing every aspect of that paper, and then adding other materials which, although quite different in texture, echo the same qualities and tone as the paper itself.

An example of such enhancement is shown in the charming 'Chesspiece Knight' collage photographed here. Newspaper is a wonderful and inexpensive source of material. It is used in a highly decorative manner for the knight, so as to show to full advantage the many variations of newsprint—from tightly printed

Above: Sprayed watercolour or diluted ink makes an interesting splattered effect. Dip an old toothbrush in the liquid, hold over the paper to be decorated and stroke the bristles with a knife. Draw the knife towards you or you will spray yourself.

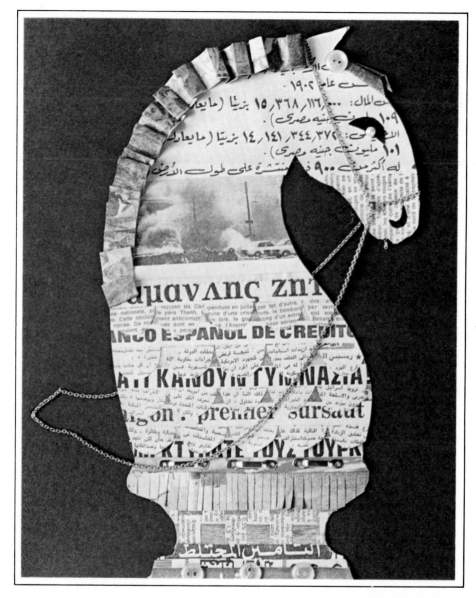

Left: 'Chesspiece Knight'
decoratively reveals some of the
subtle variations of newsprint.
Alternate dark and pale areas are
cut in different shapes and ways,
then highlighted with a few
accessories taken from
jewelry and sewing boxes.

dark areas and bold headlines interspersed with white, through grey photographic areas, to creamy white spaces.

The paper is pleated, scalloped, fringed and double folded for added interest and the non-paper details (bits and pieces taken from sewing and jewelry boxes) make delicate finishing touches. The broken chain necklet, trouser hooks and eyes, shirt buttons, pearl and scraps of sandpaper harmonize with their background— nothing jars. Their colours reiterate the creamy, grey, black newsprint tones, and they seem to fit quite naturally into this decorative composition.

Coloured tissue collage

Collages of coloured tissue paper are great fun and easy to make: children as well as adults will derive pleasure from this form of picture making, since little skill at handicrafts is needed to make a pleasing design. The basic method involves gluing down layers of torn or cut tissue paper of different shapes and colours, some overlapping and some not, on to a surface such as a piece of hardboard. Even a first attempt by a beginner can have rewarding results. Tissue paper, one of the most popular of decorative papers, has many artistic possibilities because its delicacy and translucency allows for a subtle blending of colour and a variety of shapes.

Pictures may be abstract, representational, with or without a definite structure, according to your personal taste. You will become more skilled with practice and will eventually find that you know how to achieve a desired result, rather than laying down the paper in a haphazard way. Many famous painters, such as Matisse and Picasso, have turned to collage with tissue paper as another form of expression, with beautiful results.

Shape and colour

Often the most interesting shapes can be obtained by tearing rather than cutting the tissue paper. Jagged mountain peaks, stormy seascapes and cloud effects can all be produced by tearing the paper carefully. The tearing method is, however, only suitable if your design is composed of fairly large pieces of paper. Smaller pieces are better cut, especially if you wish to use geometric shapes or if your design requires straight edges for its effect—for example if you are producing a picture of a building. The jungle scene illustrated here is made from cut papers and the result is more detailed than it could be if only torn papers were used. You can use co-ordinating or contrasting colours for your picture, depending on the subject. It is a good idea to experiment with the material before embarking on a picture. Tear small pieces of paper and stick them down on a small piece of white cardboard. Overlap some of the pieces to see the changes in colour. Well-placed over-

---

Tissue paper collage

You will need:
Tissue paper in various colours.
Non-toxic white glue thoroughly mixed with the same amount of water.
Hardboard is probably the best kind of board to use if the work is intended to be permanent. It is light-weight but rigid, and does not buckle or warp on contact with water. White canvas board, illustration board, or stiff cardboard of required size are also suitable. In fact the technique may be used on any surface to which the glue and water solution will adhere: glass, plastic, wood and metal can all be used as well as hardboard or canvas board.
A primer or sealer for applying to porous surfaces before you start, so that they will take the glue.
Cloth or soft tissues for blotting excess glue.
25mm (1in) wide flat acrylic fibre brush.
Pencil.
Scissors and ruler (optional).
Clear polyurethane varnish and paintbrush (optional).

Left: 'Jungle Scene' in which the designer has used many layers of paper in small cut pieces, creating a richness of colour which vividly conveys the lushness and depths of jungle vegetation.

Opposite: 'Johnny Appleseed' uses torn and wrinkled papers of different sizes. The papers have been 'bled' where a blending of colours was required.

lapping of papers helps to create the design and gives a feeling of depth to the picture. Using tissue papers in light colours will impart a mood of lightness and delicacy. The more layers you overlap, the deeper and richer the colour will become. If you use dark-coloured papers they will appear black when overlapped. Use the collages shown here simply as a guide when making your own: do not try to copy them too closely as it would be extremely difficult to reproduce them exactly.

Gluing the papers

The tissue paper is glued to the chosen surface with white glue which will not show through the tissue. A solution of half glue and half water is used: a strong adhesive is not necessary to stick down such light papers. The procedure for gluing is always the same. Having torn or cut your first piece of paper to the size and shape your require, place it in position on the board. Lightly mark its position with a pencil to indicate the area of the board over which to spread the glue. Remove the tissue paper and brush on the glue. While the surface of the board is still wet, place the tissue in position, gently pressing it in place; then brush more glue over the surface of the tissue to coat it with a protective film, removing any air bubbles as you work. Do not remove small wrinkles in the paper as these will add texture to the design. Continue to add pieces of tissue paper in this way until your design is complete. (You can begin by covering the entire board with an uncut sheet of tissue paper, if you wish. This will have the effect of making the particular colour occur in different hues throughout the picture.) To ensure that no part of the board is visible, take the tissue paper beyond the edges of the board and glue it down round the sides and to the back.

The water in the glue solution will not make the colour come out of the paper and bleed on to the adjacent paper. However, if you want to encourage the colour to bleed, creating interesting effects, dip the glue brush in a little more water and apply to the edges of the glued paper.

When the picture is finished and the glue is dry, apply another coat of glue to the entire surface of the picture, as a protective covering. When this coating of glue is dry, place the picture (unless it is on hardboard) under a weight overnight, in order to flatten it. The water in the glue solution may have buckled the board slightly. If the board is still not flat, glue a sheet of paper all over the back of the board to straighten it. If a more permanent protective covering is desired, use a clear polyurethane varnish to coat the surface. This has the advantage of preventing fading.

Crackers

Cracker making and decorating

In the first half of the nineteenth century, Tom Smith, a British sweet-maker, visited Paris. Impressed by the way Parisian confectioners wrapped their bon-bons in paper that was elegantly twisted at both ends, he decided to improve on his own sweet [candy] wrappings. First he added a love motto and larger more decorative wrapping papers. Then he included a small gift and sandwiched a friction strip of saltpetre between the layers of paper. When pulled, the strip went off with a bang. Thus, in 1840, the ingenious idea of the cracker came into being.

The success of the cracker was immediate. As popular with adults as with children, crackers were something to be enjoyed all the year round. No celebration was complete without them—engagement, wedding, birthday and christening parties, public holidays and anniversaries as well as Christmas—and specially designed crackers were often introduced to commemorate memorable events. This idea of making special crackers to suit the occasion seems worth reviving and, since they are not difficult to make, designing and decorating your own personalized crackers could prove a very enjoyable project.

Above: Crackers are fun to have at parties. Children particularly enjoy the snap of the banger and finding small gifts inside.

Materials and tools

It is possible to buy all the materials required from cracker maker suppliers: bangers, mottoes, tiny gifts for fillers, stiffening card, lining paper, crêpe paper, motifs for surface decorations and formers. Alternatively, you may prefer to buy only bangers from the suppliers, choose your own papers and fillers, and make a pair of formers for yourself.

Formers are the essential tools for cracker making and are hollow tubes rigid enough to retain the cylindrical cracker shape throughout the making process. If you make your own, use plastic drain piping or a similar firm tubular material 4cm (1½in) in diameter. Cut one piece 12.5cm (5in) long and the second 25cm (10in) long. If your formers differ from these traditional measurements, you will have to adjust the size of your cracker papers accordingly.

Decorative outer wrappings are usually made of crêpe paper but plenty of other papers, ranging from newspaper to gift wrapping paper, are just as suitable. The only essential quality is 'tearability'. Cut a piece of paper into an oblong, with the grain running lengthwise. Roll into a cylinder, then pull apart. If it tears quite easily, your paper has passed the suitability test.

Lining paper should be quite thin. White tissue paper, airmail writing paper and flimsy typewriting paper are all suitable.

Stiffening cardboard is rolled to make the firm central cylindrical shape of the cracker. Use a fairly thick but pliable cardboard, such as is used for cereal boxes.

Fillings   The little gifts that go inside crackers can be almost anything you choose—from a solid gold swizzle stick to a plastic whistle—providing they are not dangerously sharp, highly inflammable, extremely fragile or too large to pass through the diameter of the formers you are using.

Basic crêpe crackers

Single crêpe is traditional cracker paper and the best with which to make your first crackers. A roll of crêpe paper generally measures about 50cm by 260cm (20in by 102in) and will make 16 crackers. (The left-over crêpe can be cut in half then rejoined with a central decorative band to make eight more crackers.)

Cut the crêpe into pieces measuring 30.5cm by 16cm (12in by 6¼in), with the grain running parallel to the longer side. Cut the lining paper into pieces measuring 28cm by 15cm (11in by 6in) and the stiffening card into pieces measuring 15cm by 9cm (6in by 3½in).

Basic crêpe crackers
You will need: Crêpe paper. Lining paper. Stiffening cardboard. Bangers. Mottoes (optional). Fillings. 1 metre (39in) string. A pair of scissors. Ruler, scissors and clear general purpose glue.

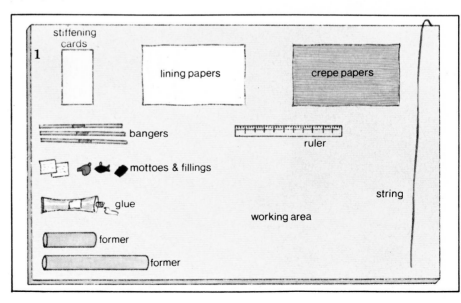

1. A neatly arranged work table helps to make your cracker making more efficient.

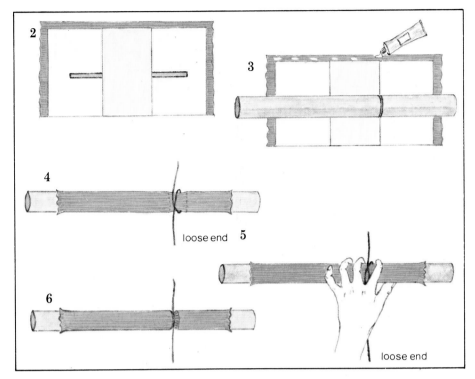

loose end 5

loose end

2. *Bottom edge of crêpe and lining paper are neatly aligned. Motto and banger go on top and are covered by the stiffener card, which is placed vertically with the bottom edge aligned with the crêpe and lining paper.*
3. *Correct positioning of the formers is essential.*
4. *Small former is moved to leave a gap precisely 3.5cm (1⅜in). Loop the string loosely around the cracker and let it lie dead centre in the gap.*
5. *Hold both formers with the left hand, letting the string lie between index and second finger. Loose end of string is under the wrist ready to be pulled by right hand.*
6. *Push the small former back to its original position to firmly crease the choke. Then remove the former completely and untie the string.*

Lay the papers in neat piles on your work table. Add the mottoes, bangers, fillers, formers and glue (fig. 1). Assembling your materials neatly like this will help greatly towards the efficiency of your cracker making. Anchor your string to the table leg on the far right-hand corner and place the loose end of the string facing you across the table (fig. 1).

Frill the short ends of one piece of crêpe paper by stretching the ends lightly with fingers and thumb. Lay it horizontally on the table. Place a piece of lining paper horizontally on top of the crêpe. Line up the bottom edges of both papers leaving 2cm (¾in) of crêpe visible along the top edge. Centralize a banger and motto on top of the lining paper, and place a piece of stiffening card vertically on top (fig. 2).

Spread a few small dabs of glue along the edge of the visible strip of crêpe and place the formers together, the small one on the right-hand side, so that they meet precisely along the right-hand edge of the stiffening card (fig. 3). Holding all the materials together, roll them over the formers as tightly as possible making a tube shape. A little pressure at glue points will ensure the crêpe is secured. A tight tube shape and well-glued papers are important. Keeping the large former firmly in position, gently ease the small former 3.5cm (1⅜in) to the right. If the paper is too thick for you

55

to see through, you should be able to feel this gap. Accurate measuring is very important.

Now make the choke. Centralize the string over the gap. Draw it over the tube towards you, underneath and then over towards you again. Keep the string quite loose at this stage (fig. 4). Hold the cracker with your left hand, spreading your fingers so they grasp both formers (fig. 5). Let the loose end of the string lie between the index and second finger as shown. Take the loose end of the string in your right hand and pull tight, simultaneously pulling the cracker towards you with the left hand so that, in effect, the string is pulled tightly and evenly from both directions. Press the small former back to its original position abutting the larger one (fig. 6). Then remove it completely but on no account allow the larger former to shift or fall out because it is almost impossible to replace without damaging the cracker. Untie and remove the string. Then slip the filling down the large former into the cracker. Ease the former out a short way and check that the filling is in the stiffening card central area of the cracker. If necessary use something long and thin, such as a knitting needle, to push the filling out of the former and into the cracker proper. Turn the cracker round so the former is on the right-hand side. Gently ease the former out with your right hand until there is a gap of 3.5cm (1⅜in) between it and the stiffening card. Now make the other choke, using exactly the same method as before but treating the tube of card as though it were the second former.

Adding surface decorations

Plastic and foil papers, most wallpapers, flocked papers and materials like hessian [burlap] and nylon netting do not pass the destructibility test and therefore cannot be used in any of the ways described so far. They can, however, be incorporated in your crackers providing their use is strictly confined to covering the central cylinder only, never the part that is to be pulled to pieces, that is the chokes. This type of decoration should be cut to size and stuck in position after the cracker has been made up. The firm central cylinder of the cracker offers an ideal surface on which to stick or pin ornamental motifs. Use self-adhesive gift ribbon to make ornate butterfly bows, make tiny bouquets from flowers you have pressed and dried, or use decorative cut-outs from paper doilies, flower seed packets and photographs.

A look round your local stationers and haberdashers will suggest lots of other attractive and relatively cheap ideas: scrap reliefs, sticky-backed initials in metallic paper, sequinned motifs, miniature sprays of artificial flowers or fruit, or gummed paper shapes.

Adding frills to festive crackers

Once you master the basic technique of making and decorating crackers, you will feel confident and able to extend the art of cracker making. The frills and extra embellishments suggested here' are simply added to the basic crêpe crackers already described, but the results are very rewarding—unique and spectacular crackers quite unlike shop-bought crackers. Children like essentially colourful and dramatically simple designs. They are eager recipients of crackers and likely to be especially delighted if their crackers are ingeniously designed to echo the theme of a party.

By altering the traditional trumpet-shaped cracker ends and experimenting with additions to the central cylindrical shape, a cracker can be transformed into all sorts of objects. For instance, pipe-cleaner legs and lacy paper wings will turn crackers into honey bees, butterflies and creepy-crawlies from the insect world; while cardboard wheels and funnels can be used to make trains and steamships.

Clown crackers
You will need: Basic white crêpe crackers.   Coloured crêpe paper and white cardboard.   Coloured cardboard, preferably a metallic finish.   Decorative adhesive tape, preferably with a metallic finish.   Pre-gummed geometric paper shapes.   Button thread.   Paper adhesive and a pair of compasses.   Ruler, pencil and scissors.

Clown crackers

These simple but charming crackers would be a particularly suitable choice for a party using the circus as its central theme. A child could make the faces while you prepare the frills.

Cut a piece of crêpe paper measuring 70cm by 20cm (27in by 8in) with the grain running parallel to the short ends of the paper. Frill the long ends by stretching the edge of the paper with fingers and thumb (fig. 1). Lay the piece of crêpe horizontally on the work table and fold it widthways so that the bottom frill is 11.5cm (4½in) deep and the top one is 8.5cm (3½in) deep. Stick decorative adhesive tape along the edge of each frill as shown (fig. 2).

Place thread in the crêpe fold. Gather the frills as tightly as possible and tie them round one of the chokes of the basic white cracker. Separate the frills, which should be substantial enough to stand the cracker upright (fig. 3).

Cut a circle 9cm (3½in) diameter in white cardboard, decorate with pre-gummed geometric shapes to make the clown's face and stick into position on the central cracker cylinder close to the frilled choke (fig. 4). Finally, make the hat from a fan-shaped piece of coloured cardboard. Draw two 15cm (6in) long lines meeting at a right angle. Set the compasses at a radius of 15cm (6in) to form the arc, and cut out your card accordingly (fig. 5). Roll the card into a cone shape. Glue along the overlap and stick together. Place two small dabs of glue inside the cone hat and stick the hat into position over and around the undecorated trumpet-shaped cracker end (fig. 6).

Dinner party crackers

Don't think that crackers are for children only. Sophisticated and beautifully designed crackers can add to the glamour of your dinner-party table and give great pleasure to every age group. Used in place of the more conventional vase of flowers, crackers can make a pretty table centrepiece. Individually labelled and placed by each setting, they can act as place names for your seating plan. In either case, crackers can provide a delightful means of offering each guest a small gift.

1. Stretch the edge of the paper lightly to frill the long ends.
2. Stick decorative adhesive [cellophane] tape along the edge of each frill.
3. Gather the frills around one of the chokes.
4. Stick the clown's head into position.
5. Make the clown's hat from coloured cardboard.
6. Complete the hat and stick in position.

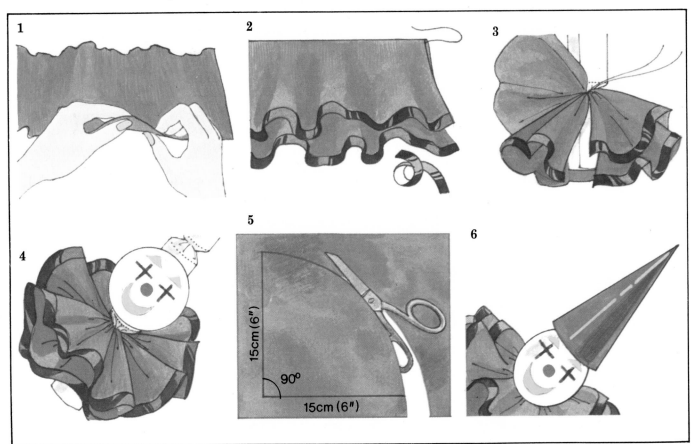

Left: Brightly coloured clown crackers will look delightful on a tea table at a children's party.

Japanese papers

Decorating with Japanese papers

Japanese hand-made art papers are among the most beautiful made today. They range from fibrous textured papers with strong, natural colours, to the most fragile 'lacy' papers which look like delicate lace. The papers are made either from wood pulp or cotton fibres and are therefore of a high quality. Japanese

Left: Some samples of Japanese papers. From the top they are 'Stars', 'Scallops', 'Net' and 'Daisies'.

craftsmen guard the secret of the lacy paper formula so that this paper is relatively rare.

Sometimes extra fibres, dried leaves and flowers, pieces of gold leaf and butterflies are embedded in the pulp. These are usually translucent and are shown to best advantage when light shows through them, as in mobiles, screens, lampshades and window decorations. Some papers have such wonderful variations in fibre colours that definite designs such as apples, fish and dragons can be identified in the fibre dyes.

These papers can be bought from specialist art shops and some handicraft shops and stationers. They are sold by the sheet—measuring about 1m by 65cm (39in by 26in). As they are often quite fragile they should be stored flat or carefully rolled between protective layers of other paper to prevent tearing or creasing. If creases occur, iron gently with a cool iron.

As you might imagine, the names of the various Japanese papers are as exotic as the papers themselves—the lily candle holder was made with Koto Buki, and the mobile with natural Ogura. Other lacy types include Rakasi Hana-Asa and Rakasui, while a simple brown textured paper is called Sugi Kawa.

Making a mobile

A disc mobile is an excellent first project for using Japanese hand-made papers. It is quite simple to make and shows off the full beauty of the paper.

Soak the wood shavings in water for about 30-40 minutes or until quite supple. Using a craft or handyman's knife against a ruler, cut the shavings into strips of varying lengths—from about 10cm to 30cm (4in to 12in) but about 2cm ($\frac{3}{4}$in) wide in every case. The mobile in the photograph is made up of 26 circles, although of course you can make as many as you like.

Curve each strip into a ring. Secure each overlap seam with a paperclip, lay it on its rim and leave to dry. Remove the paperclips and stick the seam of each wood shaving with adhesive. Using the point of a darning needle make small holes on opposite sides of each ring. The holes should be just large enough to be able to thread the fishing line easily.

Place blotting paper or old newspapers on a firm flat surface and place a sheet of the Japanese paper on top. Spread a little adhesive along one rim of each wood shaving ring and stick down on to the Japanese paper. Place the rings close enough to each other to avoid wasting too much paper. Allow sufficient space between them to enable you to cut them out easily afterwards. When the adhesive is thoroughly dry, cut away surplus paper with small

---

Making a mobile

You will need:
1 sheet white Japanese paper such as Ogura.
1 sheet coloured Japanese paper such as Sugi Kawa.
2 strips natural wood shavings.
A piece of bamboo about 30cm (12in) long.
8.5kg (19lb) nylon fishing line, 2m (6ft 6in) long.
A piece of string, about 60cm (24in) long.
Clear adhesive.
Paperclips, ruler.
A darning needle.
Handyman's or craft knife or a pair of scissors.
Strips of wood shavings, natural or coloured—usually about 4cm (1½in) wide and 80cm (31in) long can be bought from many craft and handyman's shops.

scissors so that the paper discs fit the rings exactly.

Cut the fishing line into four pieces of differing or equal length according to your taste. Tie a knot at the end of one piece of fishing line. Put a tiny dab of glue on the knot. Thread one of the discs on to the line and push it down gently until the wood shaving rests against the knot. Thread the remaining discs on to the fishing line, placing them at intervals and in colour patterns of your choice. Always stick the discs on to glued knots. Tie the loose end of each piece of fishing line on the bamboo, again securing the knots with adhesive. Tie ends of string to each end of bamboo stick, tie and hang up in a light place.

Water-lily candle holder

Milliner's wire is another material which makes an excellent frame to support delicate light-weight papers and this decorative candle holder is not difficult to make. For safety's sake, however, it is essential that—either before or after making up—the paper is sprayed with flameproofing spray. Milliner's wire can be bought from haberdashery shops and binding wire from florists and some craft shops.

Unwind about 35cm (14in) of milliner's wire. Curve the wire so that the loose end touches the 35cm (14in) mark and cross the wires at this point to make a loop. Secure the loop with a twist of binding wire but do not cut the milliner's wire. Unwind another 2.5cm (1in) of milliner's wire before making a second loop the same way and the same size as before (fig. 1). Secure the loop with binding wire as before. Continue making loops at regular

Opposite: This lampshade is made of Japanese paper with leaves and butterflies embedded in it.

Right: A water-lily candle holder makes an elegant table decoration.

1. Make two loops of wire, securing with a twist of binding wire.

intervals the whole length of the milliner's wire without ever cutting it, and securing each loop with a short length of binding wire.

Cut the paper to the approximate shape of the loops. Spread a little adhesive around one rim of each loop and stick the paper to it. When completely dry, trim the paper neatly to size. Spray the paper with flameproofing spray.

At this stage the loops are still loose and the next process is to straighten them. Coax the strip into a spiral allowing ample space in the centre to stand the candle. Use binding wire to secure the spiral in two or three places and use your hands to cup the flower petals gently into a pretty shape. The number of turns in the spiral will of course depend on the size of candle used. A fat candle, as shown in the photograph, standing alone or on a saucer of the same diameter will be encircled by three layers of petals—a total of about 40 petals.

Butterfly lampshade

Artificial light is also very effective for showing off the special qualities of Japanese papers, and the iridescent colours of butterflies' wings glow prettily at night in this lampshade. Choose a very low watt (not more than 60w), pearlized [soft-white] bulb and a simple lamp base which does not overpower or distract the eye from the delicate tracery of the paper shade.

Paint the lampshade frame with the gloss paint and leave to dry. (If the frame is already white this is, of course, unnecessary.)

Measure the four oblong panels that go to make up the lampshade frame and cut a pattern for each in newspaper or other rough paper. Hold them against the lampshade frame to test for accuracy, then use as templates to cut out your Japanese paper. Cut on the generous side to avoid the possibility of any unsightly gaps at the side struts. A small overlap of paper panels is a good idea and you will need a little extra length for pulling taut. Any real surplus can be trimmed to size once the paper is stuck on to the frame. Spread a thin line of glue down the two side struts and those parts of the top and bottom ring that go to make up one panel. Carefully position the appropriate piece of Japanese paper and stick it on the frame. Attach at the top first, then the sides, gently pulling the sheet taut from the bottom, and finally affixing the bottom. Trim off surplus, and repeat the process for the remaining three panels of the lampshade. When quite dry, spread a thin band of adhesive on the outside of the paper shade close to the top ring of the frame and gently press the velvet ribbon trim into position; similarly attach ribbon to the bottom of the shade.

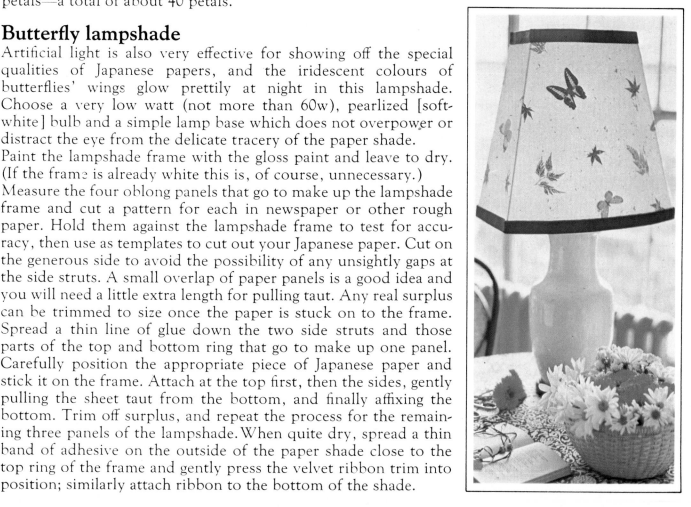

Paper flowers

Tissue paper flowers

Artificial flowers are not new; the beauty of real flowers has always been a source of fascination and attempts to copy them over the years have been ingenious and varied. All sorts of different materials have been used, including wax, shells, glass, china, wood, felt, wool and many different kinds of fabric and paper. Artificial flowers are now most commonly made in paper—they are easy to make and have great decorative appeal, and there is still scope for those with a serious interest in flowers to achieve accurate results.

Look at a real flower

Before beginning to make flowers, it is important to know how real ones are constructed. A cross-section of the components of a flower, with the main parts and their names is shown here. Although you can make satisfactory and decorative flowers by learning some useful papercraft techniques, you may wish to go a stage further and make some that are closely copied from nature. It is then important to know exactly how a flower is formed by taking it apart and noting the exact number of petals and where they are placed, the shape of the calyx and the distribution of the stamens. Whatever kind of flower you are making, it is a good idea to incorporate some accurate botanical details—they make the flower more interesting and subtle.

Tissue paper

Tissue is ideal for the beginner. It gives good results without requiring a great deal of expertise in handling, and the colours available are pretty enough to give the flowers the glow and fragility of real ones. A 'rainbow' variety is also available which gives an attractive effect to flower petals. The quality of tissue paper varies from flimsy to firm: it is worth buying the best available because it gives better, more lasting results. Tissue paper does have certain disadvantages, however, in comparison with crêpe paper, although this is more difficult to handle initially. It cannot be shaped in the same way, and if it becomes over-

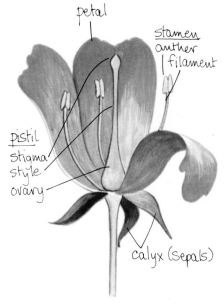

Above: A cross-section through a composite flower showing its main parts.

67

handled or crumpled it may lose its bright crispness. It also fades rather quickly when exposed to sunlight, so arrange the completed flowers in an attractive container placed well back from the window, and direct some lamplight through them in the evening. Take care not to get tissue paper wet; even a few spots of water can cause the dye to run and spoil the paper.

Flower-making equipment

The only other materials required are wire and stem covering. Florists' wire is a very fine wire used for securing the flower to the stem, and galvanized wire in various thicknesses is used for stems.

Right: Delicate tissue paper peonies in a colourful arrangement.

Wire stems can be covered with strips of green crêpe paper, but rubberized garden tape can also be used. Only the most basic equipment is necessary—a pair of good quality sharp, pointed scissors with a blade about 6cm (2½in) long, a pair of wire cutters (the sort used for electrical repairs) and a PVA glue or a paste.

To make tissue peonies

Peonies are large, striking flowers that vary in colour from yellow, white and magenta to all shades of pink and red. The dark red varieties are the most familiar, but there are delicate two-shaded flowers in tones of white and gold, pink and cream, and pale and deep pink that look particularly subtle made up in tissue paper.

Cut off the required number of galvanized wire lengths for stems and straighten them out.

Each sheet of tissue paper measures about 50cm by 74cm (20in by 30in). Divide each sheet into six equal squares by folding the paper in half and then into three. For each flower you will need three squares of one shade for the centre petals and three squares of the other colour for the outer petals. Take a tissue square and fold in half, in half again and in half once more, making the creases as sharply as possible (figs. 1–3). Finally, fold the triangle into an irregular cone shape as shown (fig. 4).

The next step makes the shape of the petals, so take care to make the cut exactly as shown (fig. 5). Cutting line A indicates the shape of the inside petals, cutting line B the outside petals. Cut three of each. Spread out the petals but do not flatten them (fig. 6). Dab a spot of glue on to the centre of each of the petals (fig. 7) and place them one on top of each other (fig. 8), taking care to keep the creases in.

Take a stem wire and bend the top over to prevent the petals from falling off (fig. 9). Push the wire through the centre of all layers of petals (fig. 10). Push the centre of the petals close to the wire so that a 'trumpet' shape is formed (fig. 11). Hold it in place with your finger until the glue begins to hold. Secure the base of flower by binding tightly with florists' or green plastic-covered wire (fig. 12). Shape the flower by gently separating each of the layers of outer petals and turning them downwards, and by separating the inner petals and leaving them standing vertically (fig. 13).

Cover the stem wire by cutting a strip of green crêpe paper about 2.5cm (1in) wide and wrapping it very tightly round the base of the flower. A dab of glue on the end of the paper may help to hold it in position (fig. 14). Rotate the wire, and wrap paper strip in a bandaging movement down to the bottom of the wire (fig. 15). Break off the paper and secure the end with a spot of glue (fig. 16).

Tissue peonies
You will need:
Sheets of tissue paper in the colours of your choice.
25cm–35cm (10in–15in) of 1.25mm (18 gauge) galvanized wire.
Florists' wire or green plastic-covered wire.
Green crêpe paper.
PVA glue or paste.

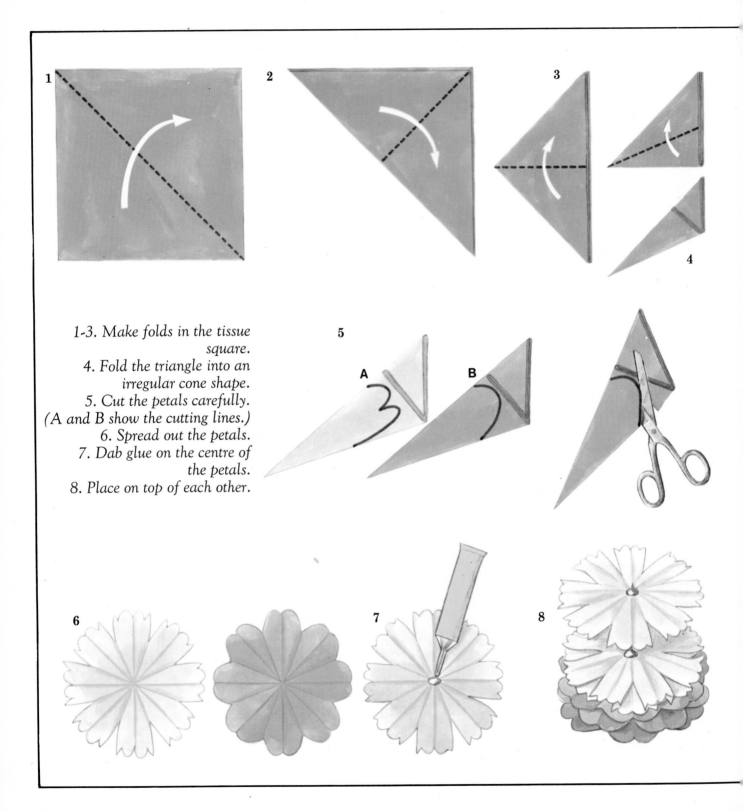

1-3. Make folds in the tissue
square.
4. Fold the triangle into an
irregular cone shape.
5. Cut the petals carefully.
(A and B show the cutting lines.)
6. Spread out the petals.
7. Dab glue on the centre of
the petals.
8. Place on top of each other.

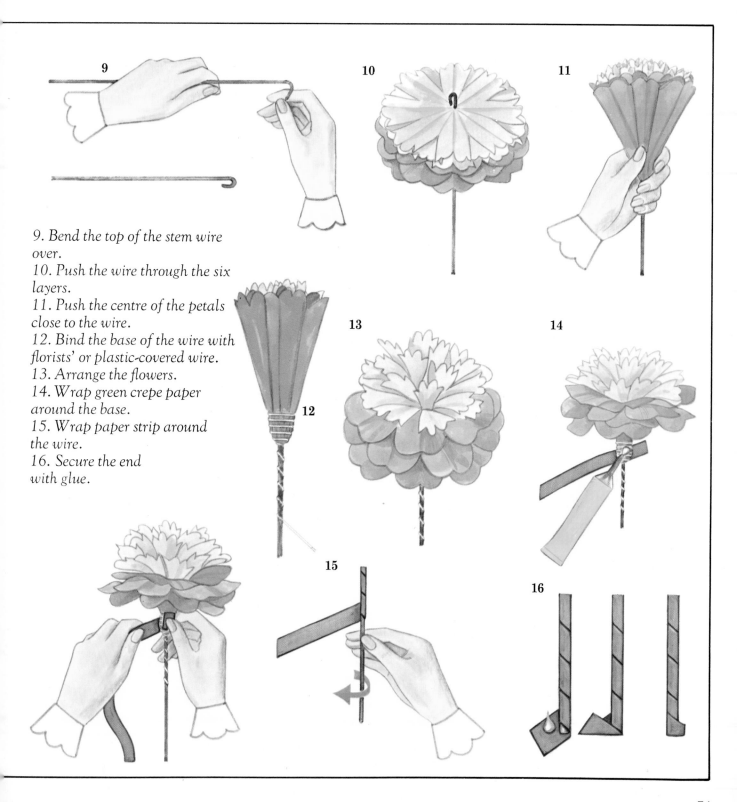

9. Bend the top of the stem wire over.

10. Push the wire through the six layers.

11. Push the centre of the petals close to the wire.

12. Bind the base of the wire with florists' or plastic-covered wire.

13. Arrange the flowers.

14. Wrap green crepe paper around the base.

15. Wrap paper strip around the wire.

16. Secure the end with glue.

Making flowers in crêpe paper

Crêpe paper has always been popular for making flowers because it can be stretched and formed to suit whatever flower shape you like to make. It has quite different qualities from tissue paper and the more time you spend coaxing and shaping it the more interesting it becomes. Even the cheapest brand of crêpe paper will expand over half as much again, which gives plenty of scope for modelling flowers—from roses to arum lilies. It is also easily wrapped around wire to make a perfect covering for stems.

Crêpe paper is bought in lengths of about 3m (10ft) and this is sometimes called a fold. The kind generally available is single crêpe which is 50cm (20in) wide. Crêpe paper is also manufactured especially for flower-making in two layers bonded together, 25cm (10in) wide, and this is known as double crêpe. Unfortunately, it is now sold through very few outlets.

Preparing flower parts

Cutting a crêpe paper strip   Crêpe paper stretches one way only—lengthways. The grain, that is the small lines, run along the width. The petals and leaves in most flowers have the stretch going across and the grain running downwards. Hold a fold of paper firmly in one hand and, with the other hand, cut strips off with sharp scissors—parallel to the edge of the fold (fig. 1) and cutting across the grain. For stem bindings cut strips 12mm ($\frac{1}{2}$in) to 2.5cm (1in) in width. For petals cut 10cm (4in) widths for small flowers and 15cm (6in) widths for medium sized flowers. Always cut crêpe paper strips across the grain to ensure that the stretch goes in the right direction.

Covering wire with crêpe paper strips

When practising this technique the wire will not be attached to a flower but, when you are actually flower making, it could be. First put a little glue at the top of the wire or, if it is attached to a flower, around the base of the flower and calyx (fig. 2). Wrap the binding around the top of the wire very tightly two or three times. Holding the paper between the thumb and forefinger of either the left or right hand, twirl the wire round with the other hand. Guide the binding diagonally down, stretching the paper to make it tight. When you reach the bottom, break off the paper, glue and stick down.

Cutting fringes

Cut a crêpe paper strip as described, making it the width you want the fringe to be plus 2.5cm (1in) as a base for attaching to the stem wire (fig. 3). Unfold the strip and fold it in half, fold it again, then fold it once more. Pin it once or twice to keep it in place. Start cutting the fringe along the grain, making the cuts about 12mm ($\frac{1}{2}$in) apart or closer if you want. You can leave the ends of the fringe square or cut them into points. There is an alternate way of cutting a fringe. If your hands are fairly strong and your scissors are sharp you can cut a fringe straight into the crêpe paper strip without unfolding it. This is obviously the quickest method and one worth trying when you have more confidence and experience.

1. Cut strips of folded paper.
2a, b, c. Secure and twirl the binding around the wire, sticking it at the base.
3a, b, c. Cut out a fringe along the grain leaving the ends square or cutting them into points.

73

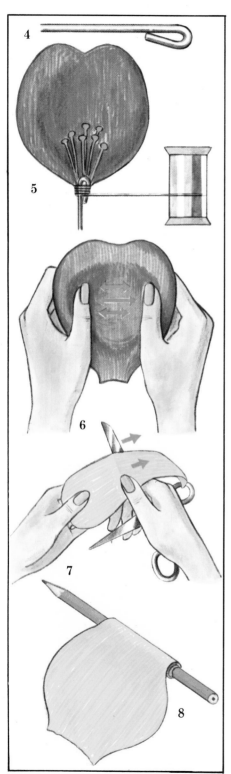

Assembling the flower

Bending the wire top   The top of the stem wire is often bent to prevent the flower centre and petals falling off. Take the top of the wire between thumb and forefinger, turn it over 6mm ($\frac{1}{4}$in) and bend it back as close to the wire as possible. This is easier to do with a pair of pliers (fig. 4).

Wiring petals on to stem wire   This is done with florists' wire and takes a little practice. You may find it helps to put a little glue

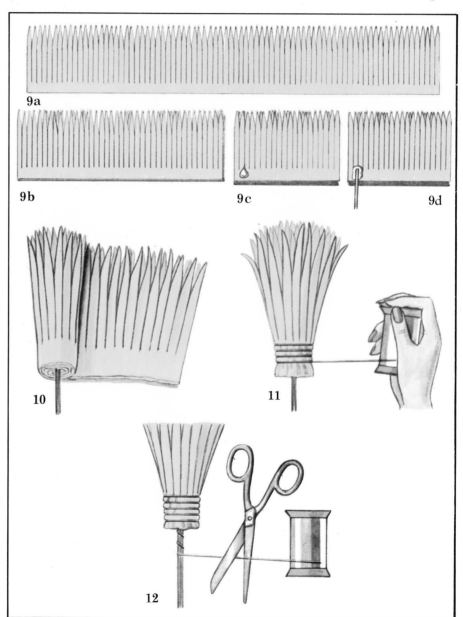

at the base of the paper before you start. Hold the paper (whether it is the centre of a flower, or petals) against the stem wire, wind the florists' wire round a few times and hook the end of the stem wire over the wound wire to secure it (fig. 5). Pull very tight and continue winding round and down the stem a little way before breaking off.

Shaping petals

Cupping petals for shape   Place your thumbs and fingers on either side of petal. Stretch the paper widthways gently with your thumbs, producing a cupped shape (fig. 6).
Shaping petals with scissors   Hold the petal with one hand and the opened scissor blades in the other. With the inside of the scissor blade behind the paper, gently scrape across the underside of the paper, as shown (fig. 7), to give a gentle curve.
Curling petals around a pencil   For a tighter curve, wrap the petal edge round a pencil or orange stick very tightly, then withdraw it (fig. 8).

Artichoke flowers

These are one of the simplest types of crêpe paper flowers to make and you can use the same techniques to make many different types of flowers. The centre is composed of several strips of fringes that have been wrapped around the stem wire. The fringe ends have been pinched and ruffled up to soften their outlines. These flowers make amusing and attractive decorations and mix well with dried grasses.

To make centres   Cut a strip about 16.5cm (6½in) wide, as described in preparing flower parts, from each of mauve, white and yellow folds of paper. Unwrap each, cut fringe and cut each into three equal pieces. These are now ready to wrap round the centre of the flower. (Some strips will be left over for use on the next flower.) Take a yellow fringe piece and fold into four. Put a dab of glue on the base and place the stem wire on the glue (fig. 9). Making sure that the base of the crêpe thicknesses are flat and level, roll the paper round the wire (fig. 10). Secure in place with florists' wire (figs. 11 and 12).

Continue to add fringed strips—first white, then mauve, then yellow. You can stop at three strips or use a fourth strip if you want the flower centre to be larger.
To make the outer petal   Cut a 23cm (9in) wide strip from the brown or green paper. From this strip cut off four 61cm (24in) lengths. Refold three of the four lengths. Take the first folded length and trim 2.5cm (1in) off the width to make a 20.5cm (8in)

Artichoke flowers
You will need: 4 folds of crêpe paper—suggested colours are 1 mauve, 1 yellow and 1 white for the centre and 1 brown or green for the outer circles of petals. This is enough for two flowers. 50cm (20in) of 1.6mm (14 gauge) stem wire and green crêpe paper. Florists' wire. Large tube of PVA glue. Tape measure.

Assembling the flowers
4. Bend over the top of the stem wire.
5. Wire the petals on to the stem wire.
6. Stretch the petals gently widthways to produce a cupped shape.
7. Shape the petals with scissors.
8. Curl the petals around a pencil.

Artichoke flowers
9a–d. Fold fringe piece into four. Glue the base and position the stem wire.
10. Roll the paper around the wire.
11, 12. Secure in place with florists' wire.

wide strip. Trim another one to 17.5cm (7in) and the fourth to 15cm (6in). These form the four circles of outer petals.

Fold each strip neatly in concertina folds about 3cm (1¼in) wide and, when you have done about 10 folds, stop and trim off the excess with scissors. Cut a pointed shape as shown (fig. 13). Unfold the strips, then bunch the base into tiny pleats as shown (fig. 14). Also shape the petals by cupping. Working with the 23cm (9in) wide strip, put dabs of glue all the way along the base and lay the flower centre down on the glue (fig. 14). Wrap the petal strip firmly in place at the base (fig. 15). Hold it for a few seconds until the glue sets, making sure you keep the flower circular and even (fig. 16). Continue in the same way with the 20.5cm (8in) strip, followed by the 17.5cm (7in) strip and then the 15cm (6in) strip, keeping the base even but graduating to shorter petals on the outside (fig. 17).

13. *Cut a pointed shape from a concertina fold strip.*
14. *Unfold and bunch the base into tiny pleats; glue base and lay flower centre down.*
15. *Wrap petal firmly in place.*
16. *Hold carefully while glue sets.*
17. *Repeat with other strips, graduating the petals.*

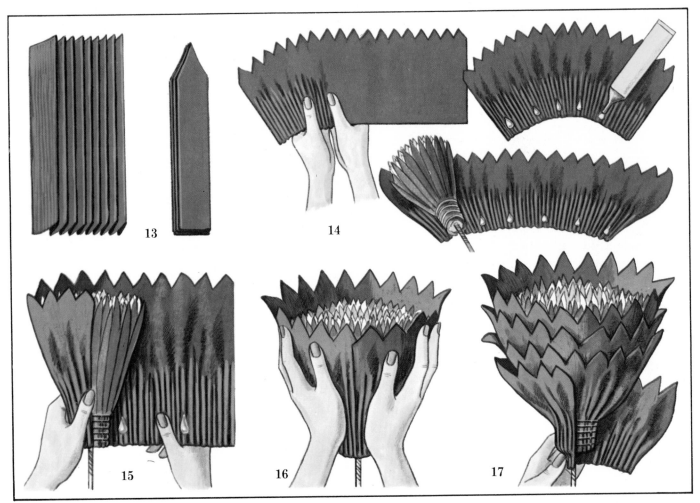

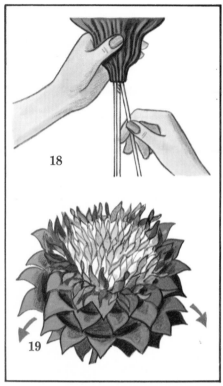

18. *Lay two new wires against the first wire, pushing them up into the flower base.*
19. *Flatten the points of the petals firmly down and out.*

Left: The completed artichokes in a simple arrangement.

Strengthen the stem by adding two more stem wires. Lay the two new wires against the first wire, pushing them up into the flower base (fig. 18). Cover the wires with a 5cm (2in) wide crêpe paper strip as described in flower-making techniques, pulling the strip really tight.

The final touches   Ruffle and spread out the centre fringes and twist them together with your fingertips. Work the crêpe paper a little to make it look more natural. Flatten the points of the petals firmly out and down (fig. 19). The final stage is to curve the stem slightly towards the top near the flower.

Realistic paper roses

Here, you will see how to make lifelike paper roses which are constructed in a similar way to real ones. The petal patterns have been closely copied from nature and each flower is made up of about 26 petals—although a real rose will often have many more. The flowers illustrated have been made from single crêpe paper in order to achieve the most realistic effect. You could also try making them in tissue paper, using the same method but omitting the petal-shaping procedure.

Old-fashioned roses

These roses have been made in white, with green for the calyx, leaves and stems. They have been lightly tinted with a little oil paint to give them extra, subtle colouring. This is quite simple and if you wish to do the same thing, you must add a few more materials to your shopping list.

Petals   There are two sizes of petal patterns to make. Smaller roses have about 24 petals cut from the small pattern and the bigger roses have 16 small petals and about eight to ten large ones

---

Old-fashioned roses

You will need:
Single crêpe paper in white and green—a fold of each makes several roses.
26cm (10in) of 1.25mm (18 gauge) wire for stem wires.
Florists' wire.
Yellow stamens or sisal string and yellow powder colour.
PVA glue and paper scissors.
Small tube of rose madder oil paint.
White spirit.
Sable brush—medium size is best.

1a, b. Trace patterns for the petals.
2. Bind stamens to the stem wire.
3. Pin petal patterns to the paper.
4. Curl the edges of the petals.

Right: The completed rose, carefully copied from nature.

1a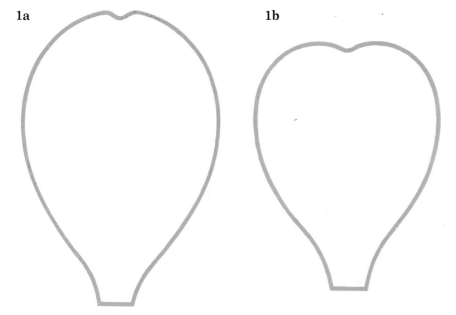

1b

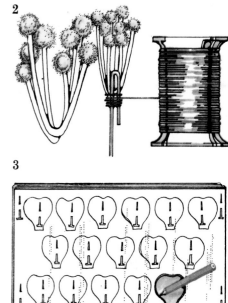

2

3

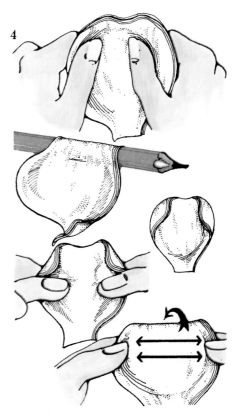

on the outside of the flower if you prefer this size.

Stamens If you are using string, unravel and straighten a length from the ball, then cut off about 2.5cm (1in) for each flower. Dip the tips of the string in a mixture of PVA glue and yellow powder colour.

Trace the patterns in figs. 1a and b on to thin paper and stick them down on light cardboard, such as a cereal box. When dry, cut out and label them.

Bend over the top of the stem wire for 13mm ($\frac{1}{2}$in). Fold a few stamens in half and bind to the stem lightly with florists' wire (fig. 2).

First cut the fold of white crêpe paper in half. Unwind one half and fold that in half, then again, then once more. You now have eight layers which you must hold together by pinning at each corner. Draw round the petal patterns lightly with a pencil, as close together as possible, then pin each drawing in the centre (fig. 3). Use tiny pins if you have them. Prepare the quantity you will require for all your flowers and cut them out carefully.

To shape the petals take a group and remove the pin. Take four petals and shape them all together, as shown under general flower making techniques. Cup the centre, curl the edges over a pencil and gently stretch the curls (fig. 4). Make enough petals for at least one complete flower.

To fix the petals on the stem take four prepared petals and separate them. Cup and shape each one a little more. Lay them down in a line so that they overlap and pleat the lower edge as shown (fig. 5). When overlapping the four petals in a line, dab a blob of glue at the bottom of each one. Allow the glue to set a little then pick them up together and wrap them round the stamens and stem wire. Secure with florists' wire (fig. 6).

Do the same with four more petals, wrapping them round the inside petals in a continuous spiral. Do at least 16 petals in this way (fig. 7), spreading the petals further apart as you reach the outside of the flower. Continue adding petals until you are satisfied with the shape of your flowers.

To make the calyx, stems and leaves trace off the calyx pattern and cut calyx pieces from green paper, cutting one for each rose (fig. 8). Shape the calyx by stretching across the base of the points and rolling the tips between the fingers. Dab the base with glue and stick round the bottom of the flower (fig. 9). Cover the stem wire with narrow green strips of paper as described in the section on general flower making techniques. Curve the stem wires. If you like the effect of a few leaves, add some to the stem, cutting them smaller and more pointed than the petals.

White spirit [petroleum spirit] must be used as the medium when colouring crêpe paper as water causes it to disintegrate. Pick up a minute quantity of oil paint with the brush and, working on a tile or pottery saucer, dilute with white spirit [petroleum spirit]. Make sure to mix them very thoroughly, then brush a little on to a spare piece of white crêpe paper to test the colour. Add more spirit if it is too dark and more paint if it is too pale. Paint the flowers all over with the wash. Make the centre of the roses a little darker with stronger colour and add this same dark colour to the tips of the calyx, the stems and leaves. After painting, place the flowers near an open window to help get rid of the strong smell of the spirit, but don't worry about this as it will disappear in a day or two.

5. Overlap and glue the petals.
6. Secure petals to the stem with the wire.
7. Wrap and spread the petals realistically.
8. Make one calyx for each rose and shape and stick in place.

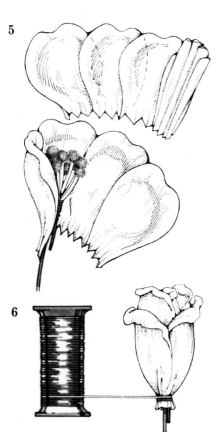

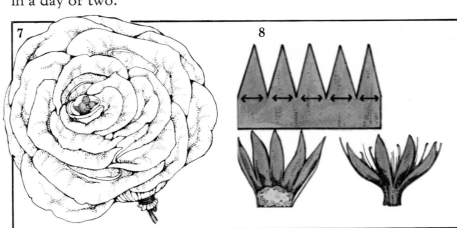

Decorative boxes

Making your own boxes

There are so many different uses for attractive cardboard boxes. Longlasting boxes made of strong cardboard and fitted with compartments can be used to keep jewelry or to display a treasured collection of shells. Less durable boxes can add glamour to a gift or add to the value of something made for a bazaar—cakes, sweets [candies] or biscuits. They can even be hand-printed to give a present a truly individual touch. Boxes of exactly the same shape will look quite different when decorated. Try flock paper, wrapping paper, magazine cut-outs, old maps, foil paper or fabric to make them more attractive. You can varnish boxes to protect them and add gold or silver motifs and decorations.

Scoring

Most heavy paper and cardboard is made up of layers, rather like a sandwich. The aim of scoring is to cut through one of the outer 'bread' layers, leaving the rest intact (fig. 1). Once the cardboard has been scored it can be bent accurately and this is the essential technique to learn when making boxes. To score, mark the line to be cut in pencil, then draw along the line lightly with a razor-sharp cutting tool, such as a scalpel, against a metal ruler. Be sure to keep your finger behind the cutting blade.

If too much pressure is put on the cutting tool and you have cut too deeply, the cardboard will simply divide in two. On the other hand, if the cardboard is scored too lightly, it will not bend successfully. A little experimentation will soon reveal how much pressure to use with different sorts of cardboard.

Suitable cardboards

Boxes can be constructed out of varying thicknesses of cardboard, depending on the type and size you are making. Small boxes with flaps should be made of cardboard about the thickness of a cereal box. Thick cardboard, such as mounting board, is not recommended for boxes with flaps because the flaps tend to drop off quickly, being attached only by a thin scored layer of cardboard. If using thick cardboard with a colour-coated surface for a

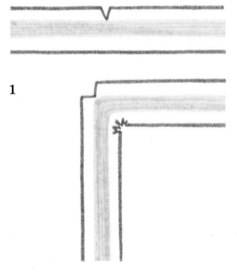

1

1. Cut through the layer of card so that it bends easily.

box without flaps the scored lines will show white, so use the type which is coloured throughout unless the box is to be covered on completion. You can begin making boxes out of any stiff paper or cardboard at hand, but there are many suitable cardboards on the market which will probably make a better job of it.

Glues

When it comes to sticking boxes together, PVA wood adhesive is recommended for working with cardboard, and rubber solution is the best thing for sticking down paper coverings. There are several animal-based glues on the market which are designed especially for paper work. A thick mixture of wallpaper paste can also be used for sticking heavy wallpaper coverings, but it will cause bubbles to form on thin paper and can make the cardboard bubble if it is too liquid.

Making the boxes

One piece boxes In this type of box, the lid is virtually an extended flap. Draw the pattern in fig. 2 with all squares equal in size. Draw round a square object to create a square or use a protractor to measure the angles exactly ensuring that they are all 90°. Cut along solid lines; score along dotted lines. Fold and stick as in fig. 3a and b.

This pattern can be easily adapted to other proportions (fig. 4). The main point to remember is that the sides must all be the same depth and the lid must match the base.

2. Cutting and scoring diagram of a square one-piece box with lid. 3a, b. Fold and stick to assemble the square box. 4. The pattern adapted for an oblong box.

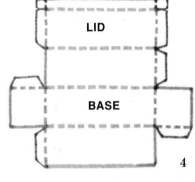

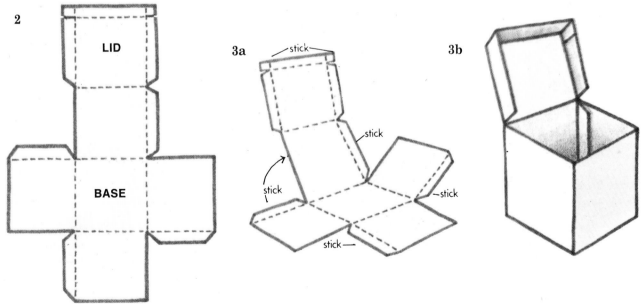

Puzzle boxes

This set of boxes which can be twisted and turned to produce six different pictures is really less complicated than it looks. It is constructed out of four, square, one-piece boxes.

Right: A set of four 'puzzle' boxes can be twisted to make six different pictures.

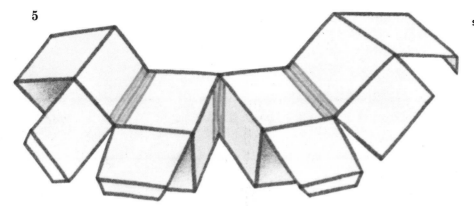

5

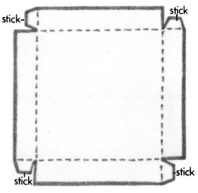

stick

stick

stick

stick

6

Make four square boxes with attached lids (omitting side flaps on lids). Be sure that the boxes are very accurately made. Hinge them together with transparent adhesive tape as shown in fig. 5. Find six suitable square pictures and cut them into sets of four equal squares. Stick each set of four squares to the relevant sides, one at a time, until the puzzle is completed.

Boxes with separate flapped lids

Make a separate lid by cutting the pattern as in fig. 6. Cut along solid lines; score along dotted lines. Draw the centre square 1.6mm ($\frac{1}{16}$in) larger all round than the base of box so that the lid will fit over it. Stick flaps inside lid.

Covering boxes If attractive cardboard is not available you can use something easily obtainable such as a cornflake box and cover it in attractive wrapping paper. When covering boxes with decorative papers, remember not to stick the covering to the flap areas, or it will make the joins too bulky. Stick the covering to the box while it is still flat and assemble the box while the covering paper is still damp, when it will have more give.

Petal boxes

These charming little boxes with four petal tops and bottoms need the minimum of sticking because most of the flaps tuck neatly into one another. They are easy to make once you have learnt the principles of box making given above.

Use these boxes to hold sweets or small gifts at children's parties or bazaars. Neatly file away buttons or jewelry in them. Keep some on your desk to hold paper clips, elastic bands and drawing pins [thumb tacks].

Make them out of coloured or white cardboard and decorate them with lighthearted gummed paper motifs, cut-outs from magazines, stars, spangles, sequins or anything else you can think of. The

5. Hinge puzzle boxes so that they can be turned to show their six sides.
6. Separate lids are slightly larger all around than the base of the box.

Petal boxes

You will need:
Rough paper for pattern.
Thin cardboard measuring about 22cm by 32cm ($8\frac{1}{2}$in by $12\frac{1}{2}$in).
Pair of compasses.
Ruler.
Pencil.
Scalpel.
Cutting board.
Paper adhesive.

pattern given is for a box measuring about 9cm (3½in) by 7.8cm (3in) by 7.8cm (3in) square. To make your own size box, keep these proportions but double or treble the measurements, or reduce them by half.

Following fig. 7, cut out a trial paper pattern of rough paper first, as this will save precious cardboard. Draw the figure to the measurements shown, lightly indicating scoring lines. To make accurate circular tabs, draw a square, the sides of which measure half the length of the top of one of the sides of the box (fig. 7). Point A is half-way along one of the sides of that square as shown. Draw a circle from point A, with its radius half the length of the

Below: Coloured pieces of cardboard pasted with wrapping papers have been used for these attractive petal boxes.

sides of that square. Score lightly along the orange dotted lines from underneath because they are valley or sunken folds, and score lightly along the brown dotted lines from above because they are mountain or peak folds. Fold to form the box, at the tabs. Fold down the top and bottom of the box. Glue the base.

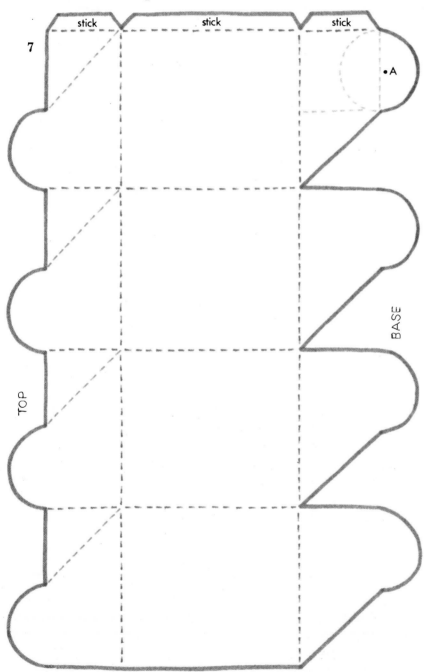

7. *The petal box pattern, which is cut in one piece, can be adapted to other sizes.*

Taped boxes with separate lids

Details of the sort of cardboard to use for box making, the techniques of scoring, cutting and sticking boxes and the importance of ensuring that all angles are 90° have already been given. You will need all this information to make the following boxes.

Square boxes with lids

Draw the pattern in fig. 1 on cardboard. Cut out the box with a sharp cutting tool, cutting along solid lines and scoring along the dotted lines. Fold up the side pieces on scored lines to form the box. Hold the corners together on the outside of the box with decorative adhesive tape (fig. 2).

To make a lid, draw the pattern in fig. 3 but make the centre square 1.6mm ($\frac{1}{16}$in) larger all round than the base of the box, so that the lid fits comfortably over the box. Make the side pieces as deep as you like, from 6mm ($\frac{1}{4}$in) to 2.5cm (1in) or more. Finish the lid by sticking adhesive tape all round the outside (fig. 4) or on the corners only.

It is a simple matter to adapt the pattern to make an oblong box, or one that is shallow or deep (fig. 5). The sides must be all the

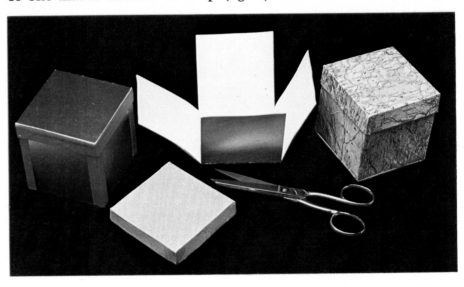

Right: Covered square boxes with separate lids are easy to make and assemble.

88

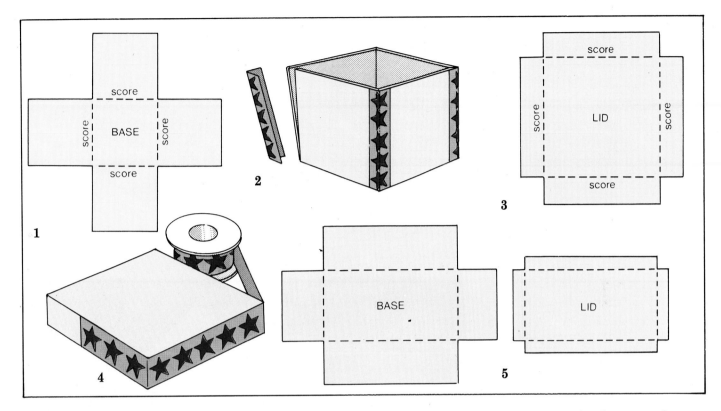

same depth and the lid must be at least 1.6mm ($\frac{1}{16}$in) bigger overall than the base.

Decorative paper cover

Lay the cut-out shape of the box, scored side down, on the wrong side of the decorative paper. Glue and press down smoothly. Don't leave the covering paper to dry out completely or the paper may tear. When the paper is almost dry, cut all around the shape (fig. 6), either right to the edge of the box or else leave a margin of 1.3cm ($\frac{1}{2}$in) at the top of the sides to be turned over. (If you do this, allow for the extra thickness when making the lid.) Gently fold up the scored sides to avoid tearing the paper.

Lining square boxes

Both bought and hand-made boxes look especially glamorous if they are lined with beautiful papers. Try a matt gold paper inside a box covered in a tortoise-shell paper, a marbled paper inside a deeper coloured box, or a plain plush paper inside a box covered in a rich, gold-embossed paper.

Cut a piece of paper the same dimensions as the box, with small tabs on any two sides. Fold in the same way as for the box and

1. *The pattern for the square box.*
2. *Assemble and hold the corners together with decorative adhesive [cellophane] tape.*
3. *The pattern for the lid.*
4. *Finish the lid by sticking adhesive [cellophane] tape around the outside.*
5. *A pattern for an oblong box.*

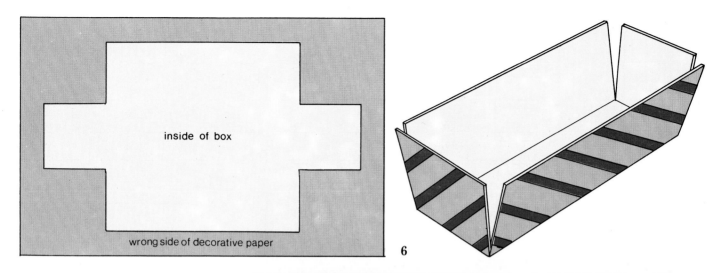

inside of box

wrong side of decorative paper

6

6. Stick the cut-out shape of the box to the decorative paper and cut around the shape. Fold up the scored sides gently.
7. Ease slots into position to make compartments.
8. For long boxes, form peaks of folded card.

Right: Rectangular boxes which have been sumptuously trimmed and decorated.

9, 10. To make round box bases, score on the dotted inner line and cut on the solid outer line. Cut out segments if cardboard base is thick, or V-notches if it is thin. Then, bend up tabs and glue to attach base to the inside of the box.

Opposite: An old shop-bought oval box covered with pretty floral paper.

stick the lining to the inside of the box by the tabs. Stick the lining to the inside of the top of the box as well. To line with cardboard cut the vertical measurement of the lining slightly smaller than the box to allow for the thickness of the cardboard.

Compartments for boxes

The easiest way to make compartments for square boxes is to cut them out of interlocking sections of card. The strips of card should be as high, long and wide as the inside of the box. Cut slots half-way up the strips and slot them into each other (fig. 7). For long boxes, make compartments of folded card, scoring the top sides of the card and the underside of the card as shown (fig. 8) to form peaks the same height as the box. Make as many compartments as you need from one long strip the width of the box, then drop it into the box.

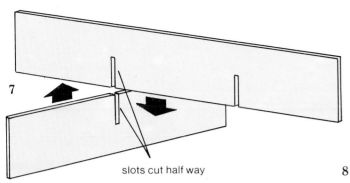

7

slots cut half way

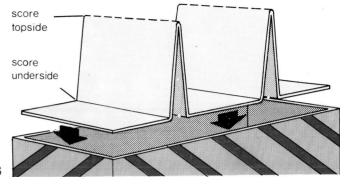

score topside

score underside

8

To make round boxes

With a pair of compasses, draw a circle on cardboard to make the bottom of the box. With the same centre draw another circle with a radius 1.3cm ($\frac{1}{2}$in) wider than the first one. Cut a straight piece of cardboard the length of the circumference of the inner circle, plus a 1.3cm ($\frac{1}{2}$in) overlap, and the height you want the box to be. Overlap the sides and stick them together to make a cylinder.

To make a base If you are using thick cardboard, score on the dotted inner line of the base circle and cut on the solid outer line as shown in fig. 9. Snip into the outer circle and remove alternate segments to make tabs as shown. Bend tabs upwards and stick to the base of the cylinder with the tabs inside the body of the box. If you are using thinner cardboard, the base can be V-notched (fig. 10).

Make the lid the same way as the base, but draw the inner circle 1.5mm ($\frac{1}{16}$in) wider in radius. Make the side of the lid about 1.3cm ($\frac{1}{2}$in) deep.

Covering round boxes

Wallpaper is suitable for covering round boxes. It comes in hundreds of attractive designs and colours and will also add strength to the box. But wallpaper will not bend sharply and should therefore be butted at the side joins and cut right up to the top and bottom edges of the box.

Most thinner papers will bend easily, so when using them cut a circle of paper the same size as the box base with an additional 12mm ($\frac{1}{2}$in) margin all round. Cut tabs 12mm ($\frac{1}{2}$in) into the circle, stick the circle to the bottom of the box, then turn up the overlapping tabs and stick them all round the sides of the box. Cut a strip of paper the length of the circumference of the box with a 12mm ($\frac{1}{2}$in) overlap. For the depth you can add an extra 12mm ($\frac{1}{2}$in) for turning over the top edge to the inside of the box or you can cut it to the top of the box only. Glue round the sides of the box covering the turned-up tabs of the base.

9

10

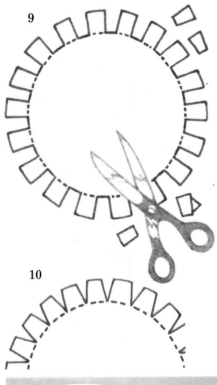

Découpage

Introduction to découpage

The word *découpage* means 'cut out' and the craft is concerned with decorating objects with cut-out paper prints or illustrations, and then varnishing them. Originally the idea was to 'sink' the print under many coats of varnish so that the print would look as though it had been inlaid in the surface of the object. This is very effective for wooden objects, such as boxes or even chairs. However, you can also decorate glass and metal objects with découpage or cover a large area such as a floor or wall entirely with prints, and in these cases the prints need not be sunk. In any case, modern varnishes have lessened the number of coats necessary, making découpage inexpensive and fun. All you need to be able to create unusual and attractive pieces is time and patience.

Découpage was a popular pastime in eighteenth-century France, when ladies of the court used to amuse themselves by copying the lacquered Chinese and Japanese furniture that was all the rage at the time. Découpage was known as 'poor man's lacquer' and, in Britain, 'Japanning'. Early in this century the craft of découpage came into vogue again, this time in America where it is still very popular. Découpage studios sell a variety of prints, varnishes and finishes many of which are exported to specialist shops and art shops in other parts of the world. Even if you do not have access to these découpage materials you can buy suitable alternatives at craft shops.

Choosing decorative prints

There are innumerable sources for attractive prints and illustrations—art shops, junk shops, sales, stationers and museums are all possibilities. Almost any prints are suitable, from catalogues or old books, to posters, wallpapers and wrapping papers, but do remember that if they are thick cardboard or paper they will be much more difficult to sink. Try to choose prints on thin paper, and to use prints of similar thickness on one object. Christmas cards and postcards can be used if you soak them in water and peel off the thick backing paper. If it will not peel off easily, you may be able to rub the backing off in tiny pellets. Don't risk soaking your favourite card as you may destroy it.

If you have a plain black and white print you can colour it with water colours, felt-tipped pens or coloured pencils. Do this before cutting it out.

Materials

The main materials used in découpage are the prints, sealer, adhesive and varnish. There is a lot of scope for using a variety of products and you should make sure that they are compatible— that, for example, the varnish you have chosen will not dissolve the sealer you have used. If in doubt, test a small area.

Sealer Prints and illustrations must be sealed to prevent glue or varnish from seeping into them. You should do this before cutting them out. You can use a commercial sealer such as a white PVA type. If this is not available, you can make your own sealer by mixing equal parts of white spirit [petroleum spirit] and varnish. Magazine illustrations have to be sealed on the reverse side as well as the upper surface, so that the print does not show through. Some magazines are printed on such thin paper that even sealing may not entirely prevent heavy print from showing. You can test for this by sealing a trial piece first, and letting it dry thoroughly before you check the result.

Adhesive The type of adhesive you choose depends on the surface of the object you are decorating. For wood, a PVA adhesive can be used. If the surface is metal or glass you should use a general-purpose glue. Wallpaper paste is an alternative which has the advantage of making the print easy to slide into position on the object.

Varnish Almost any varnish is suitable for découpage, although traditional varnishes take longer to dry than polyurethane varnishes and this can be very important when you have to apply several layers and allow each one to dry thoroughly. Both types give prints a yellowish tinge, which makes it difficult to retain a clear blue or green base colour.

There are also a number of specialized découpage varnishes. These are designed for specific projects so their suitability should be carefully checked with the mail order catalogue or the shop-keeper. They have a quicker drying time than traditional varnishes, some drying in one hour rather than twenty-four hours. They also need fewer coats to achieve a good finish.

A commerical plastic coating is a useful alternative to varnish as it gives a very clear finish which leaves the original colours virtually unchanged. It is sold in two parts, lacquer and hardening solution, which are mixed equally in a glass or ceramic container. Unlike varnish it works best when applied quite thickly, and it dries in about two hours at room temperature.

Decorating a wooden box

A small wooden box is a good object to start on and can be decorated in many different ways.

Preparation

Fill any holes or cracks carefully with a proprietary plastic wood filler, then sandpaper the whole box thoroughly. Wooden surfaces can be left with their original finish or primed and painted with emulsion paint. Make sure that the base paint goes on smoothly; any flaws in the basic foundation will show through the layers of

Decorating a wooden box
You will need: Plain wooden box. Assorted prints. Primer and emulsion paint (optional). Wood filler (optional). Sealer. Water colours, felt-tipped pens or crayons (optional). Adhesive or wallpaper paste. Fine sandpaper, sanding block. Wet and dry paper. Fine steel wool. Wax polish and duster. Varnish. Pair of large scissors, pair of small scissors with curved blades; scalpel.

Left: The pattern chosen to decorate the box overleaf. Cut out all details in the print with a scalpel, since any flaws in the cutting will show through the varnish.

95

varnish. You will need two coats to make a really good job of it. When choosing the basic colour remember that the type of varnish you use will affect it.

Sealing

Remember all prints should be sealed before being cut out (magazine illustrations on both sides): this stiffens them and makes them easier to cut. Paint on the sealer thinly and evenly, covering the whole print.

Cutting out

The cutting out is very important as every tiny detail will show

Below: The care and patience taken to decorate the box has been worthwhile. It would make an ideal present.

through the varnish on the finished box. It is therefore worth taking a lot of trouble at this stage. Cut away any white surround with the large scissors first, then cut the details with the small curved scissors. With the curve turning away from the direction you are cutting, you make a slightly bevelled edge which gives a smoother surface for the varnish. Leave any fine detail until last so that it doesn't get damaged while the rest of the design is being cut. Then cut it out carefully with a scalpel.

Put the cut-out design in a safe place until you are ready to stick it down.

Sticking down

Cover the back of the print evenly with adhesive and press it down on the box with your fingers. Working from the centre outwards, smooth the print so that no air bubbles remain and no print surfaces overlap. Make sure that all the edges are properly stuck down so that varnish does not seep underneath. Wipe off excess adhesive and allow to dry.

Varnishing and sandpapering

The drying times and number of coats of varnish vary, and the point at which you decide the object is finished—or even whether you wish to sink the design—is obviously a matter of personal taste. Broadly, a traditional or polyurethane varnish will need up to 20 coats to make an embedded finish, while a specialized product will only need up to eight coats and a plastic coating about six. If you are using a traditional or polyurethane varnish you should sandpaper between all coats following the tenth coat since sanding at an earlier stage could damage the prints. The special découpage products and the plastic coatings can be sandpapered between every coat.

Clean the surface of the box first to get rid of dust and fluff. Brush on the varnish evenly, taking care to catch all runs before leaving it to dry. Work in a good light so that you can see any runs. If they do occur, allow the varnish to dry and then sandpaper the uneven spots before putting on the next coat. When sanding the surface between coats, use fine sandpaper wrapped round a sanding block. For a very fine finish, wet and dry paper is the best to use. Wash all surfaces with soap, rinse and dry thoroughly before the next coat of varnish.

Finally, for a really glowing finish, and to get rid of sanding and brush marks, rub down the surface with wet and dry paper and then with fine steel wool. Wash, rinse and dry, then wax polish the box until it shines.

Decorating with découpage

There is no limit to the area you can decorate with découpage. With immense patience and innumerable prints you could, in theory, decorate an entire room; découpage floors, like the one shown here for instance, can look superb. In fact, the découpage base may be made of almost anything with a hard and durable surface: glass, metal, ceramics and even plastics are suitable.

Right: There is no limit to the area you can decorate with decoupage. This patchwork floor has a most unusual effect.

A découpage screen

A screen composed of three or more panels is also a suitable subject for découpage, and planning and decorating one so that it is totally covered with pictures can be a very rewarding project. The finished screen can be displayed on a wall, as in the photograph, or used as a traditional room divider. The Victorians and Edwardians were particularly fond of découpage screens and used to cover them with decorative prints, pictures from newspapers and magazines, and greetings cards. The numerous coats of varnish or shellac over the pictures gave them a yellowish glaze.

If you look in antique shops and sale rooms there are still many fascinating old prints to be found. These need not be in good condition as you will probably be cutting them up anyway. Alternatively, you may prefer to use modern designs and pictures, from posters, newspaper clippings, wrapping paper, greetings

Below: The completed decoupage screen, used as a wall panel.

To make panels you will need:
Hardboard cut to the size of each panel.
Wooden battens 50mm by 25mm (2in by 1in) for each panel, three times the length and three times the width. (These strengthen the back of the hardboard and prevent warping.)
A woodworking adhesive.
Panel pins [slim nails] 20mm ($\frac{3}{4}$in).
Hammer and screwdriver.
Decorator's size.
A hand saw.
Screen hinges which allow the panels to fold both ways. Two hinges per join, and screws.
Chisel.
Gloss paint, primer and paint-brush (optional).

cards, wallpaper and from many other sources. You could start with plain paper of simple design as a base and add borders or friezes of cut-outs. If you are using wallpaper, make sure it is not too thick, since it will create an uneven surface. Remember that prints used should be of a similar thickness in each project. When you are planning your screen, it often helps to decide on a theme or a group of colours. Make sure that you have enough prints to cover the area—you may need more than you think—and that you have a good variety. Light and darkness, interest and drama are important elements for a large area such as this, which can easily look monotonous if there are not enough contrasts. If you are using an old, fabric-covered screen as a base for découpage, remove any tacks, strip off the fabric covering, rub down the frame and attach pieces of hardboard to it; otherwise construct your own frame.

Making the panels

Saw the battens into the correct lengths and glue and nail them together and then to the rough side of the hardboard (fig. 1). Allow the panels to dry flat, away from direct heat. Keep them flat during all stages of your work. Coat the hardboard and frame with decorator's size to seal it. Chisel out an area the size of each hinge on the battens. Screw on one side of each hinge only (fig. 2).

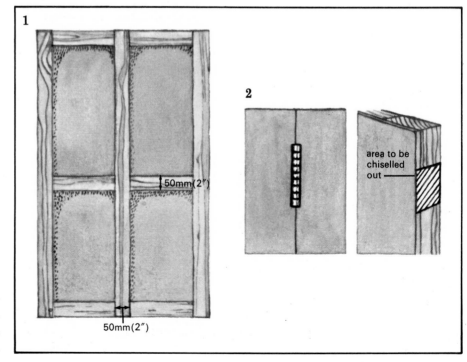

1. Position the battens on the panel.
2. Affix the hinges.
3. Mark the position of the prints.
4. Work over the edge of the screen.

Decorating the screen

Cut out the prints carefully as discussed previously. With each panel flat on the floor or a table, move the prints around on them until you are satisfied with their layout. Cut away the parts of the design which overlap: the double thickness would be more difficult to cover with varnish. Mark the position of each piece in chalk or pencil on the board (fig. 3). You could number the back of each piece and mark the same number on the area where it will be. Then its place on the board can be easily found when gluing. Starting from the centre and dealing with one print at a time, glue the prints evenly and stick them down. Make sure that all the edges are firmly stuck down, particularly if you are using glue, since the varnish could seep underneath. Roll out any air bubbles with the wallpaper roller and wipe away any excess glue. It is best to work right up to and over the edges of the screen (fig. 4).

Dry the panels thoroughly in an airy room, keeping them flat. The adhesive must be absolutely dry and the prints perfectly stuck down at the edges before you start to varnish.

Varnishing   Using long, even strokes, brush on a thin coat of varnish. Work as quickly as possible and try not to let the varnish strokes overlap each other. After each coat, go round the corners and edges with a brush to prevent runs. If they do occur, sand them smooth as described previously. Rub the surface with a soft cloth to remove dust and hairs before applying each coat. Three or four coats of varnish are usually enough for this type of découpage, and will give a tough glaze which can be wiped clean with a damp cloth.

Assembling   If you like, you can prime and paint the back of the screen with gloss paint. Attach the second side of each hinge to the corresponding panels.

Other surfaces

Découpage on glass, metal, plastic or ceramic objects as with découpage on a screen, requires no sinking of the design beneath layers of varnish. Therefore fewer coats of varnish are needed and there is no sanding down between coats. You must decide for yourself how many coats of varnish will be necessary and whether to coat the whole object or just the print itself. When applying découpage to a mirror or a glass jar, it is better to coat the print only, extending the varnish fractionally over the edges, as varnish will dull the glass.

Of course, you can also apply découpage under glass. Seal the back of the print or prints with acrylic sealer or a commercial découpage product to prevent absorption. Spread glue over the

---

A découpage screen

To decorate screen you will need:

A selection of cuttings, prints etc. About 0.5 litre (1 pint) clear polyurethane varnish for each panel, or a commercial product specially designed for découpage which can be used, not only instead of varnish, but also instead of sealer and glue, since it combines these three functions. It is much quicker to use than conventional products: one coat over your prints is the equivalent of several coats of varnish.
A wood-to-paper adhesive.
Chalk or pencil, wallpaper roller.
Scissors.
A soft cloth to dust the surfaces between each coat of varnish.
A 50mm (2in) soft household paintbrush.

3

4

inside surface of the glass and place the right side of the print on the glued area. Press out excess glue from the centre of each print to the edges. When it is dry use a vinegar and water solution or compatible solvent to wipe away excess glue, since it will leave a haze on the glass if not removed. Then cover the back of the design with a coat of clear polyurethane varnish. If you wish, you can paint a background colour over and around the design. This method could be applied to a vase, plate or ashtray, or to a glass-topped table.

Right: An attaché case and jars revitalized with decoupage.

102

Bookbinding

Tools and materials

Bookbinding, the art of protecting and decorating books, is considerably older than that of printing. It dates back about 2000 years to when people began to write on separate sheets of paper, rather than on scrolls, and needed to fix the sheets together and protect them with a cover. The ancestor of today's book is the Roman codex, which was written in script and bound with cord between two pieces of wood. By the sixteenth century, bookbinding had evolved into a specialized craft, and books were usually bound with leather which was often decorated with gold and jewels.

Today, machines are used to bind books which are inexpensive and suited to the rapid pace of our lives. However, they are less durable than those bound by hand, and certainly less beautiful. Hand binding is now reserved for special books that we wish to treasure. It can be done at home quite easily, since few special tools are necessary. The simplest form of bookbinding involves putting a new cover, called a 'case', on an existing book from which the old covers have been removed. This process—called case-binding—is described here and can be used to recover tattered paperbacks, old hardbacks or to turn a new book into something special, perhaps for a gift. Case-bound books can be full bound, half bound or quarter bound, according to personal taste.

The technique of section sewing, the other important part of the bookbinder's craft, is fully explained later.

Tools

All the necessary tools for case binding are obtainable from bookbinders' suppliers and most from hardware stores, art shops and stationers.

Glue brush Either use a bookbinder's glue brush or a 5cm (2in) paintbrush. Choose a brush with a plastic ferrule, if possible, and clean it after use.

Bone folder This is a smooth, knife-shaped tool made of plastic, wood or bone, used at many stages in bookbinding, to crease folds smoothly and to burnish. A paper-knife with a rounded end can be used instead.

Knife Used for precise cutting of paper and cover boards. A shoe-maker's knife is excellent for this but whatever type of knife you use, it should have a blade at least 10cm (4in) long and a wooden handle.

Steel ruler These are usually sold with a guard for the fingers, and are essential for accurate cutting.

Below: Some of the bookbinder's tools and equipment.

Steel set square with angles of 90°, 45° and 45°. Used to ensure that all corners are cut accurately.

Scissors or scalpel The scissors should be strong with long blades, about 20cm (8in).

Materials

There is a wide choice of materials which can be used in book-binding and it is important to use the correct ones for the particular book being bound.

Binder's board This is an essential material and is covered with book-cloth to form the book's cover. There are many grades of binder's board: strawboard is a reasonable quality for beginners. Select the weight of the strawboard according to the size and weight of the book, but if the correct weight is unobtainable, use an over-heavy board rather than one which is too light. An approximate guide is as follows: for paperbacks use 400gsm (grams per square metre) (8oz) to 800gsm (1lb) board; for medium-weight books use 800gsm (1lb) to 1,200gsm (1½lb) and for large books use 1,600gsm (2lb) board.

Bookcloth is the name given to any material used on the binder's board to make the cover. The specialist materials are cloth or paper which have been reinforced with glue. Light, closely woven fabrics can be used also but thick fabrics should be avoided as they are difficult to fold. Loosely woven cloth tends to fray and allows the glue to penetrate it. You can also cover books with strong paper. Hand-made paper is especially good for this, as is marbled paper. Thin leather can also be used but is not advisable for the beginner.

Endpapers are the protective sheets at the front and back of the book. One half of each sheet is glued to the cover board and the other half is lightly attached, 'tipped on', to the book itself. Use a paper which is neither too flimsy to adhere to the book, nor too thick to look neat, and with one rough and one smooth surface. The rough side of the paper is the one to be glued. Strong wrapping paper, cartridge [heavy bond] paper or 'craft' paper (similar to brown wrapping paper but with a rougher surface which makes it more suitable for gluing) are all recommended, as is marbled paper. Thin wallpapers are also suitable.

Mull This is the stiffened, loosely woven cloth used to reinforce the spine of a book. 50mm (2in) or 75mm (3in) wide woven cotton bandages can be used instead of mull.

Glue PVA adhesive is excellent for all the gluing processes described here. It should be used thickly on boards, mull and cloth, and thinned down with water for use on the end-papers.

Binding a paperback

Most paperback books are made up of single leaves glued together—adhesive or 'perfect' bound, rather than stitched—and are therefore not very strong. A hardback binding or 'case' will make a paperback more presentable as a gift and will prolong the life of a cherished book. The instructions given here are for binding an average-sized paperback, but of course you will have to cut bookcloth, boards and endpapers to fit each book. Fig. 1 shows the various names given to the parts of a book.

Full binding

Remove the old cover by holding the text matter in one hand and bending back the front cover with the other, so that it is at right angles to the book itself. Then pull it firmly away from the spine. Do the same with the back cover. Pick away any loose pieces stuck to the spine but leave the glue.

Fold the sheets to be used as endpapers in half, with the rough surfaces outside. Lay one folded sheet on waste paper and cover with another waste sheet leaving 6mm ($\frac{1}{4}$in) showing at the folded edge. Cover the exposed edge with glue and stick on to the spine edge of the book. Rub firmly down with the bone folder to make a good crease. Repeat with the other sheet. When the glue on the endpapers is dry, glue the mull to the spine 12mm ($\frac{1}{2}$in) from the top and bottom of the book, and to the endpapers, keeping the endpapers folded close to the text matter (fig. 2).

Full binding

You will need:
1 sheet of strawboard. Its length should be twice the width of one cover plus the width of the spine plus 12mm ($\frac{1}{2}$in). Its width should be the height of the book plus 12mm ($\frac{1}{2}$in).
1 sheet of bookcloth. Its length should be twice the width of one cover plus the width of the spine plus 30mm ($1\frac{1}{4}$in). Its width should be the height of the book plus 24mm (1in).
2 endpapers, each twice the width and the same height as the pages or 'text matter'.
1 piece of mull or bandage 50mm (2in) wider and 24mm (1in) shorter than the spine.
PVA adhesive.
Few sheets of waste paper to protect surfaces while gluing.
Sheet of waste board for a cutting surface.
Tools as described.

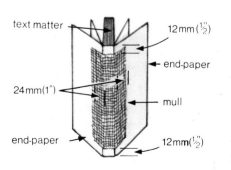

1
text matter — head
back cover
front cover
spine
fore edge
joint — tail

2
text matter — 12mm($\frac{1}{2}''$)
end-paper
24mm(1") — mull
end-paper — 12mm($\frac{1}{2}''$)

1. The parts of a book.
2. The position of the mull on the spine.

Making the case

Using the knife, steel ruler and set square, cut two pieces of strawboard 12mm (½in) longer and 6mm (¼in) wider than each cover and a strip the size of the spine. Use a piece of waste board as a cutting surface. Make sure that all corners are square and that the corners of the two main pieces match exactly.

Cut out the book-covering cloth as described. Lay the cloth flat on a large sheet of waste paper with the right side down. With a pencil, lightly trace the book measurements on the cloth to help position the boards correctly. Leave a gap of 3mm (⅛in) between the main boards and the spine piece (fig. 3). Place one board on a sheet of waste paper and work in the glue thoroughly. Make sure that the glue is even and smooth. Position the board on the cloth and stick it down firmly. Glue and stick down the other two boards.

Cut the corners of the cloth at 45° angles to the board and at a distance from the boards of twice their thickness (see fig. 3). Glue the head and tail overlap edges of the cloth, pulling the cloth firmly over the edges and rubbing down with the bone folder for a smooth finish. Glue the fore edge overlaps and stick them to the board. Smooth down carefully with the bone folder.

Attaching the book to the case

Position the book inside the case, so that 6mm (¼in) of the case protrudes at the head, tail and fore edge and so that the spine lines up with the spine piece. Holding the endpapers closed, brush glue along the top endpaper from the centre outwards, including mull. Close the case on to the endpaper, making sure that the book is square with the case. Glue the back endpaper in the same way and place the book under a weight for at least two hours, or until the glue has dried.

Titling the book

If the binding has been done simply to strengthen your book, you can use the original spine strip and front cover by gluing them on to the new cover. A transfer lettering sheet can be used on most surfaces and looks very professional.

Half and quarter binding

A book is half bound when the spine and four corners of the case have a different bookcloth from the rest of the book. It is quarter bound when it has a different bookcloth on the spine from that of the rest of the book. These types of binding look pleasing and help to strengthen the book at its most vulnerable points.

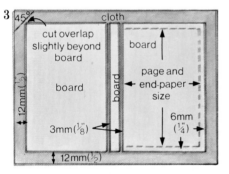

3. *The position of the boards on the cloth.*

To make a quarter binding (fig. 4a) prepare the book and cut out pieces of board as described, then cut a piece of bookcloth the width of the spine plus about 24mm (1in) either side, and 24mm (1in) longer than the spine.

Centre the spine board on the bookcloth and mark its outline with a pencil. Coat the wrong side of the bookcloth with glue and stick it to the spine piece and main boards, turning the overlaps neatly (fig. 4b). Cut two pieces of contrasting cloth or paper for the rest of each cover plus the usual overlap and so that they just overlap the spine cloth (fig. 4c). Glue these pieces to the boards and stick on the endpapers as described.

To make a half binding (fig. 5a) follow instructions for quarter binding until you have stuck on the spine cloth to the boards (see fig. 4b).

For the corners, cut four pieces of the same sort of bookcloth as the spine, with the usual overlap (fig. 5b). Mitre the corners and glue them as described earlier. Cut out two pieces of contrasting bookcloth or paper for the remaining parts of the front and back covers. Taking one piece of the cloth, place it on the front cover so that the left edge just overlaps the spine cloth (fig. 5c). Cut off the corners at the fold and glue the bookcloth to the boards. Repeat for the back cover. Finish with endpapers as described.

4a. *Finished quarter binding.*
4b. *Attaching the spine cloth.*
4c. *Covering the main boards.*
5a. *Finished half binding.*
5b. *Covering spine and corners.*
5c. *Covering the remaining boards.*

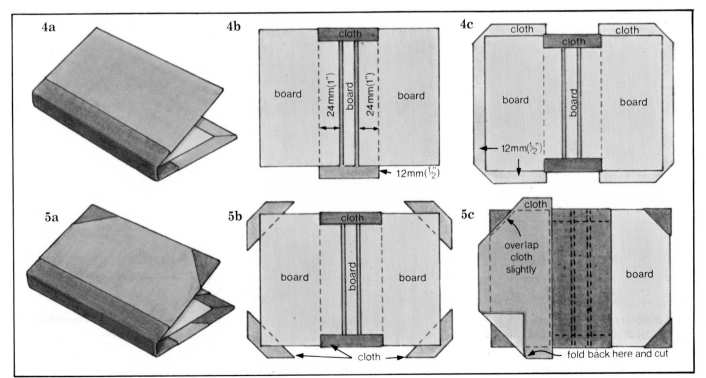

Sewing
sections together

Apart from case binding, which has been described previously, the other most important part of the bookbinder's craft is sewing. If you look at the heads of machine-bound hardback books you will generally find that the pages are divided into sections. If you open the book in the centre of one of the sections, you will see the sewing threads.

This chapter explains how to sew sections together for case binding, a technique which is suitable for books and magazines which

Right: A case for a volume of sewn magazines (upright), a single section booklet, showing the threads knotted in the centre, and two single magazine folders.

have been 'wire-stitched' (stapled) into sections, but not for books made up of single leaves glued together at the spine. You can sew several pages together to make a single section, which can then be case bound to form a booklet. This could be filled with poems, quotations, sketches, or pressed flowers. There are instructions for making your own sewing frame on page 114.

Tools and materials

As well as the tools and materials mentioned in the previous chapter, you will need several more, which are also obtainable from bookbinder's suppliers and general shops.

Dividers Spring dividers have a screw adjustment which can be set. They are used to measure the distance between the reinforcing tapes on the spine.

Needle Bookbinder's needles are strong and sharp, with large eyes. Carpet needles are also suitable.

Saw For cutting into the spine.

Tape This is used to reinforce the spine and keep the sewing sections firmly in position. It also helps fasten the sections to the covers. Stiffened linen tape is ideal but any stiff tape not more than about 1.5cm ($\frac{1}{2}$in) wide can be used.

Thread Unbleached linen thread.

Strawboard You will also need two sheets of 1,600gsm (2lb) board, measured as described on page 107.

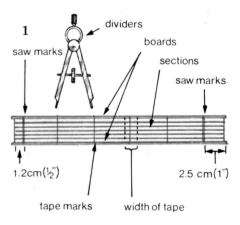

1. *Marking up the spine edge.*

Binding magazines

Binding magazines into a volume stores them for reference and provides an excellent introduction to section sewing. Do not bind together more than about eight thick magazines or 16 thin ones, or the volume will be too heavy and unwieldy.

Very carefully remove the wire staples from the magazines without tearing the paper. Put the magazines in sequence with the first issue on top. Unless otherwise specified keep the magazines in this order throughout the sewing. Using the steel ruler, set square and shoemaker's knife, cut the boards carefully to size as described for case binding. Place one board on the table or work surface. Put the magazines on the board and the other board on top of the magazines. Picking up the magazines and boards firmly with spines facing down, gently knock the spine edges squarely on the table to level them into a neat volume.

Lay the volume carefully on the table with a heavy weight on it. With a pencil mark about 1.2cm ($\frac{1}{2}$in) in from the head of the spine and about 2.5cm (1in) in from the tail. Using the dividers, divide the remainder of the spine into five equal parts (fig. 1). It

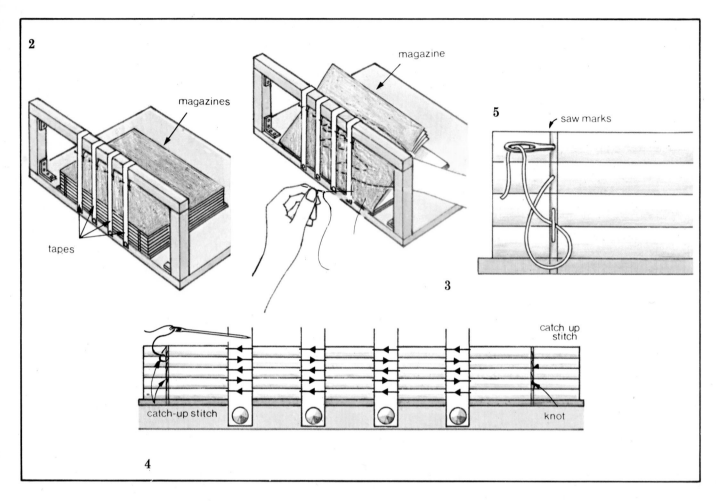

2. *Positioning the tapes.*
3. *Starting to sew the first section.*
4. *The direction in which the thread is sewn alternates with each section, as indicated by the arrows. The lower two magazines are knotted together.*
5. *Join the third magazine to the second, using a catch-up stitch. The saw marks at each end of the sections hold the stitches in place.*

may be easier to make these divisions equal if you alter the measurements at head and tail slightly, but the head measurement should always be the smaller. Make a tiny saw cut (to hold the knots) in the sections at the head and tail marks (fig. 1). Placing the tape centrally over each pencil mark, make another mark either side of the tape, so that the exact tape widths are indicated along the spine.

Sewing the sections

Before the magazines are sewn together, the tapes must be placed in position. Sewing is done around the tapes: the needle should never pass through them. You are now ready to use a sewing frame. Instructions for making your own are on page 114.

Remove the weight and top board and pick up the volume carefully, keeping the tape marks aligned. Leave the lower board in position. Then, place the volume on the sewing frame with the spine lying along the front edge (fig. 2). Cut four 25cm (10in) lengths of tape. Fix to the plywood with drawing pins [slim nails] at intervals exactly corresponding to marks on the spine (see fig. 2). Take the tapes up over the cross-piece and pin them taut. Take all but one of the magazines off the sewing frame, leaving the bottom one in the frame. This magazine is the first section to be sewn. Using needle and thread described, start sewing this section at the saw mark from the tail end of the spine. Put one hand into the centre of the magazine and thread the needle through from the outside (fig. 3). Leave about 5cm (2in) of thread hanging outside the magazine. Pass the needle out beside the first tape and pass it back into the centre of the magazine on the other side of the tape. Continue sewing along the length of the magazine to the saw mark, keeping the thread taut.

Place the next magazine (second last in the volume) front cover uppermost on top of the sewn one, aligning its marks with the tapes. Pass the needle in at the head and sew the length of the magazine as previously described. Place the next magazine (third last in the volume) front cover uppermost on top of the other two. Following fig. 4 fasten the lower two magazines together with a knot, then continue sewing the third magazine as the others. When you get to the head of the third magazine, join it to the second using a catch-up stitch (fig. 5). Sew all the magazines for the volume together, fastening them to each other at head and tail, using catch-up stitches.

When the final magazine (the first in the volume) has been sewn, bring the thread outside the spine and knot it to the adjoining magazine. Unpin the tapes and gently pull ends which were pinned to the frame base through the stitching until they are about 4cm (1½in) from the edge of the spine. Cut the longer ends so that the tapes also protrude 4cm (1½in) from the other edge.

Case binding the volume

Follow the instructions given for case binding except at the following stages.
When measuring the bookcloth allow, in this instance, about 6mm (¼in) distance between the main boards and the spine piece, since the joints need to be bigger for a volume with a wider spine. Stick the mull over the tapes to the spine only. When the glue has dried, reinforce the mull by gluing on a piece of brown craft or wrapping paper the width of the spine and 12mm (½in) shorter at the head and tail. The tapes and mull are glued down between the boards and the parts of the endpapers which are glued to the boards. Finish as described.

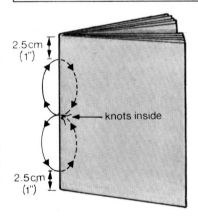

Single-section booklet

You will need:
Tools and materials as listed for case binding.
10 sheets cartridge [heavy bond] paper, about 20cm by 30cm (8in by 12in) or smaller, cut to precisely the same size.
Bookbinder's needle and thread.

2.5cm (1")

knots inside

2.5cm (1")

6

6. *The method of stitching a small single-section booklet using three holes.*

Single-section booklet

Now that you have seen how to sew several sections together and to case bind, you can make your own booklet from blank sheets of paper, in which you can write or draw. The example given here has pages made of cartridge [heavy bond] paper.

To make the section

Align the sheets of paper and fold them in half to make the central fold, with the sheets one inside the other. Mark the mid-point of the fold and push the needle and thread through it from inside the booklet, leaving about 5cm (2in) thread loose. Make the next stitch about 2.5cm (1in) from the head of the booklet. Sew through the central hole again, then make another stitch 2.5cm (1in) from the tail edge. Bring the thread back to the central hole and knot the two loose threads together, then trim the ends (fig. 6).

Making the case

The case for a single-section booklet—this also applies to theatre programmes or leaflets as well as to the handmade booklet—is made in almost exactly the same way as that for an ordinary book. However, it does not have a spine board because it is too narrow to need one.

Stick a strip of mull about 5cm (2in) wide down the inside centre of the bookcloth, leaving a gap of about 4cm (1½in) between the boards. Glue the whole of the outer sheet (two pages) of cartridge [heavy bond] paper to the covered boards as endpapers, but do not glue the spine of the booklet to the spine piece. The central 4cm (1½in) of the booklet must not be stuck. Keep the book and cover folded until the glue is dry.

Making a sewing frame

A sewing frame consists of a wooden board attached to two vertical strips of wood which are, in turn, attached to a cross-piece, as shown (fig. 2). It is essential for sewing together several sections of a book, or several magazines, accurately. The sewing frame used by bookbinders today is practically the same as those shown in early sixteenth century prints of binders. You can improvise your own quite easily.

Saw the softwood strip into three lengths, two of 12cm (5in) and one of 36cm (14in). Join the three strips as shown (see fig. 7), with the longest as the cross-piece, placing the brackets inside the four corners. Join the strips to the plywood base with the corner brackets. The frame should be firm and steady.

Making a sewing frame

You will need:
One piece of plywood or chipboard 36cm by 25cm (14in by 10in), about 12mm (½in) thick.
A strip of softwood 25mm by 25mm (1in by 1in), 60cm (24in) long.
4 L-shaped brackets with appropriate screws.
Screwdriver, saw, pencil.

7

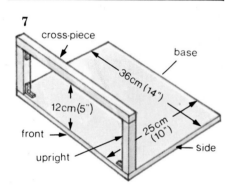

7. The specifications for making the sewing frame.

Origami

Basic
origami techniques

The word 'origami' comes from the Japanese verb *oru* (to fold) and the noun *kami* or *gami* (paper), and the craft of origami is often referred to as Japanese paper folding. Origami is a centuries-old tradition in Japan, although it is not known where in the Orient it originated.

Paper folding has always been a favourite pastime among children —there can be few of us who have not at some time made a paper hat or boat from newspaper or proudly carried home a water-lily made out of a sheet of paper from a school exercise book. Adults too can find great satisfaction in transforming a single square or rectangle of paper into a complex shape, simply by folding it in various ways. Becoming proficient in origami is less a matter of skill than of practice. There is a limited number of basic folds and, once these are mastered, there is virtually no limit to the number of designs which can be created. The designs described here are both decorative and relatively simple to make. As you progress beyond the basic steps and gain experience in the craft of paper folding you will be able to make models which spin, flap and pop, and, having copied the designs, you will probably wish to experiment with your own ideas for designs. Another attraction of origami is that it can be practised almost anywhere. It takes up little space during construction and most designs can be flattened for storage.

Papers for origami

Any paper which will crease easily is suitable for origami. You can buy Japanese paper which is specially made for the purpose, coloured on one side and white on the other. It is usually obtainable in a pack containing many squares of different colours and is widely available from stationers and art shops. Poster paper, metallic paper and patterned paper such as gift wrapping paper are also suitable, and newspaper is useful for a first attempt.

How to start

Precision and accuracy are very important requirements for

paper folding, and both elements make the craft challenging for adults. If you need a square piece of paper to create a design, make sure it is a perfect square. Firm and accurate creasing is also important. No knives, scissors or pins need be used in origami and you should always be able to unfold the paper figure back into the same square or rectangle with which you started. When folding, bear in mind the final shape you are trying to make by looking forward to the next step shown. Do not expect your first attempts always to be perfect: a second try will often proceed more smoothly than the first because, having been through the stages once, you will be able to anticipate them the second time and folding will be less mechanical.

Start by studying the symbols (figs. 1–4), The two basic origami folds are the valley fold (fig. 1) and the mountain fold (fig. 2), names which graphically describe the way in which the paper is creased. A solid arrow indicates a reverse fold (fig. 3) and an outlined arrow indicates a hidden section or a back flap which must be opened out (fig. 4).

The symbols for some of the basic origami folds.
1. Dashes indicate valley fold.
2. Dots and dashes indicate mountain fold.
3. Solid arrow indicates reverse fold.
4. Outlined arrow indicates hidden or back flap to be opened out.

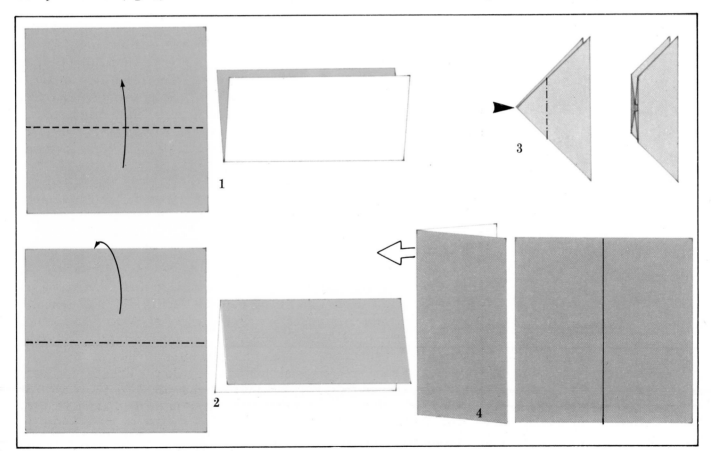

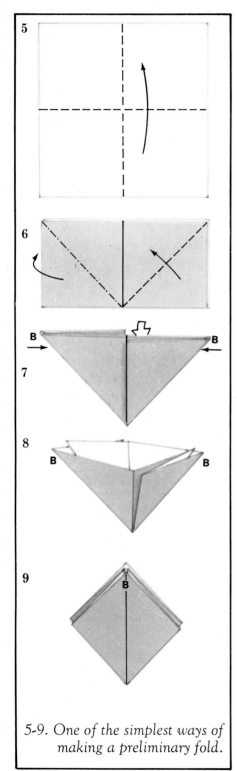

5-9. *One of the simplest ways of making a preliminary fold.*

Preliminary fold

This simple fold is so called because it is the first step in making many different models such as animals, birds and flowers of varying complexity. There are several ways of making it; figs 5–9 show one of the simplest.

Fold the paper in half vertically, then open. Fold the bottom half up to meet the top (fig. 5). Mountain and valley fold (fig. 6) to make shape shown in fig. 7. Open out model from the centre (fig. 8), pushing in the sides so that the two opposite corners B and B are placed together and facing each other. Fig. 9 shows the completed preliminary fold.

Walking penguin

For a real penguin effect, use paper which is black one side and white the other, white side up, although this may be difficult to obtain.

You must follow figs. 10–16 carefully as you read the instructions for this project.

Valley fold the paper in half from corner to corner (fig. 10). Valley fold the bottom point towards, but just short of, the left-hand point. Make a crease and return the bottom point to the position shown (fig. 11). Now bring the bottom point up again between the two layers (fig. 12), using the crease line made in fig. 11. (This is a reverse fold.) Bring the top point down so that it projects at the left-hand side. Make a crease and return to the position shown (fig. 13). Reverse fold the top point between the two layers (fig. 14), using the crease made in fig. 13. Fig 15 shows the completed penguin.

Place the penguin on a sheet of cardboard. Hold the board at a slight incline, rocking it gently from side to side. The penguin will then start to waddle forward convincingly all by itself (fig. 16).

Flower

This simple flower shape, known as *Toshi Takahama* in Japan, can be used with the leaves, which are also described, to decorate a greetings card. If you are using paper which is coloured one side and white the other, place it with the white side up. The method involves the 'squash fold', which means separating two layers of paper and re-aligning them along the creases already made.

With the paper placed as shown, valley fold the bottom corner to the top corner (fig. 17). Valley fold the side points to the top point (fig. 18). Squash fold the right-hand flap (fig. 19), so that the central fold A is positioned as shown in fig. 20. Fig. 21 shows the completed flower.

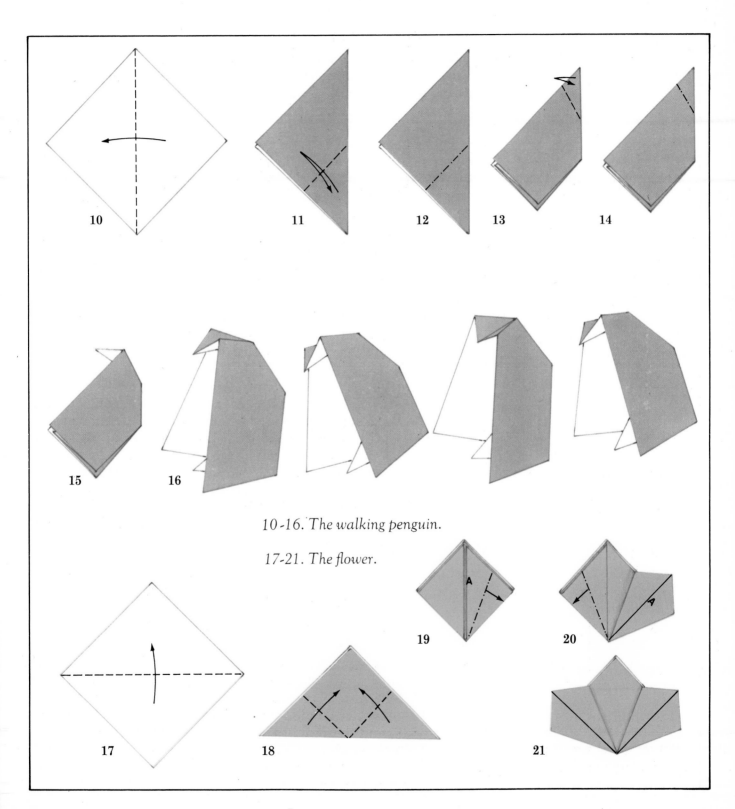

10-16. *The walking penguin.*

17-21. *The flower.*

Leaves for the flower

Use green paper placed green side up.

With the paper placed as shown, valley fold the left-hand corner to the right (fig. 22). Fig. 23 and fig. 24 show the method of preparation for the 'rabbit ear' fold—the raising of a triangular flap—which follows in fig. 25.

Valley fold the lower diagonal edge (the top layer of the paper only) to the folded edge. Having made the crease, return to the original position (fig. 23).

Valley fold the upper diagonal edge (the top layer of the paper only) to the folded edge, making a crease. Return to the original position (fig. 24).

Now bring both diagonal edges to the folded edge, using the creases made in figs. 23 and 24, pinching and raising the central corner to form a flap (fig. 25). This is known as a 'rabbit ear' fold.

Mountain fold the top point (the dark green area shown) down behind the front (fig. 26). Fig. 27 shows the flower and leaves.

Flying crane

Begin by making a preliminary fold, creasing the folds sharply. Open the paper and lay it flat (fig. 28). Valley fold edge C down to the central horizontal line laying it exactly along this line (fig. 29). Crease the fold thus formed from the left-hand corner to the fold line D (see fig. 29).

Open the paper again so that you have an additional crease line as shown (fig. 30). Repeat this procedure at every corner until the paper has all the fold lines shown (fig. 31).

Press all the sides of the paper up and in at points E (see fig. 31), to form the shape shown in fig. 32. Crease all the edges neatly so that the paper lies flat.

Turn down points F over points G, at crease lines E, at front and back (fig. 32).

With the paper positioned as shown (fig. 33), fold the front left-hand flap over the right-hand flap, so that points E touch. Repeat with the back flaps.

Turn the paper round to the position shown and pull down the top two points as indicated (fig. 34), to form the head and tail of the crane. Reverse fold one flap along dotted line H, to form the beak. Fold up the flaps along lines E to E over each side of the crane's body, and then fold them down again along dotted line J, to form wings (fig. 35).

Fig. 36 shows the completed flying crane. Make several of these and hang them by threads through point K to make a mobile.

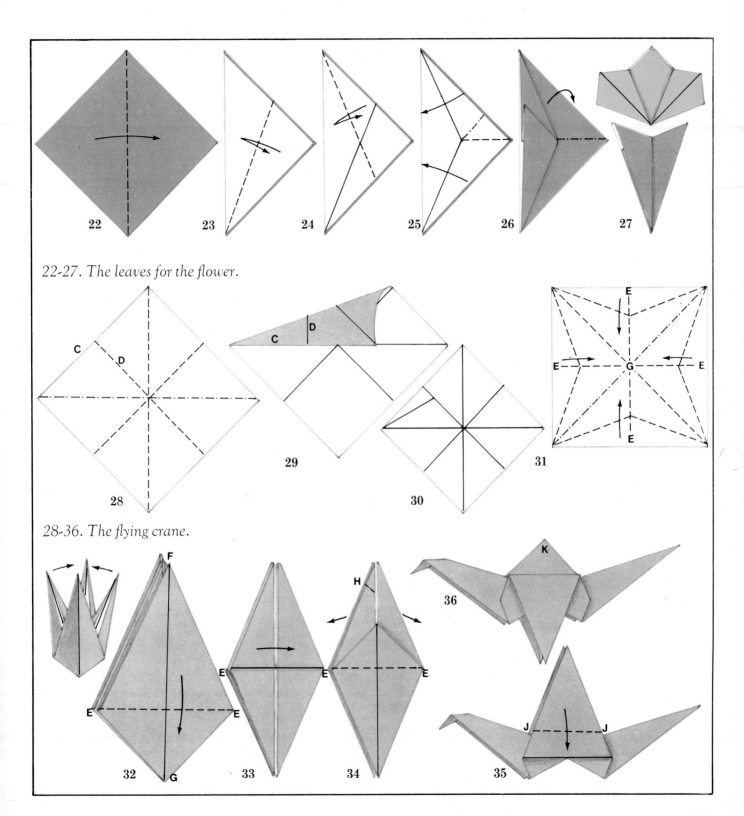

22-27. The leaves for the flower.

28-36. The flying crane.

121

More advanced designs

Here are two more origami designs— a container to hold cigarettes, bon-bons or nuts (a larger model could be used as a waste paper basket); and a delicate orchid table napkin.

A colourful container

Use a square piece of paper, about 20cm by 20cm (8in by 8in).
If the paper is patterned or coloured on one side and plain on the other, place it coloured or patterned side up, and make a preliminary fold.
With the open edges of the preliminary fold facing you (fig. 1), valley fold the top (farthermost) point down along the dotted line shown (see fig. 1). Open out. Sink the top point into the centre of the model by reverse folding the crease lines just formed into the

Below: Four colourful things to make from paper – a container, which is described here, large and small coasters and a pin wheel.

centre (fig. 2), then flattening along two facing creases to look like fig. 3. Valley fold the side flaps to the centre (see fig. 3). Repeat behind. Valley fold the top flap X up along the dotted line (fig. 4). Repeat behind. Book fold the top left-hand flap over the right (fig. 5). Repeat behind. Valley fold the upper flap Y along the dotted line (fig. 6). Repeat behind. Hold the model upside down and open from the centre (fig. 7). Flatten the inside point slightly. Fig. 8 shows the completed container.

Orchid table napkin

Use your knowledge of origami folds to make paper table napkins into orchid shapes which can be placed in wine glasses to decorate a table for a dinner party. The orchid is best made from a large napkin which should be ironed with a cool iron first, to smooth out the creases.

With the napkin opened out and placed diagonally, first fold two corners together to make a horizontal crease. Valley fold the sides along the dotted lines to meet in the middle (fig. 9). Valley fold the sides to the centre again, making firm creases (fig. 10). Now valley fold the elongated napkin in half so that the bottom point reaches the top (fig. 11). Valley fold the model in half as indicated (fig. 12). (This movement must be done with care since the paper is now several layers thick and therefore more difficult to fold).

1-8. The folds, step-by-step, for making the container.

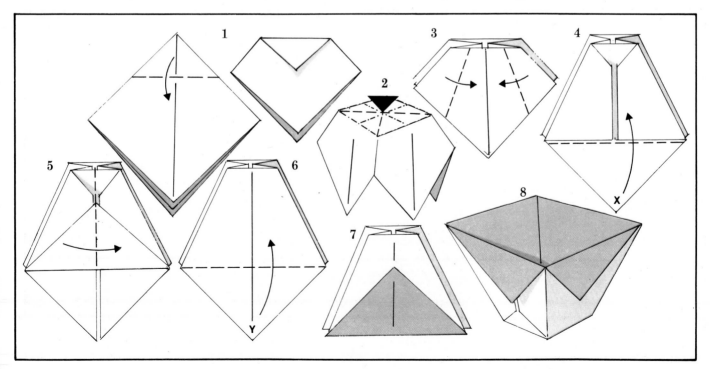

Fig. 13 shows the completed figure, seen from the side. Now place the base of the napkin in a suitable glass or goblet—one into which the napkin fits tightly so that the folds are held together. With the inside folds facing you, open out and pull down the two outer petals. Open out the central petal which is in two layers, and pull down the first layer as shown above to make a four-petalled orchid.

You could use linen napkins to make the orchids; if the napkin is ironed along each fold as it is made, this will keep the folds in place.

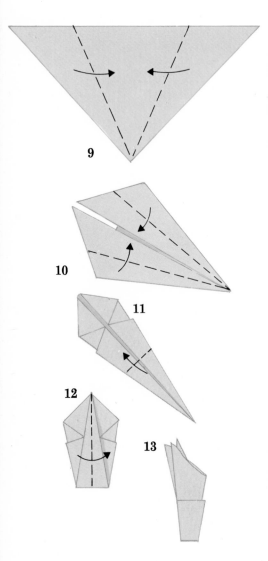

9-13. The folds for making an orchid table napkin.

Wrapping gifts

Square parcels and bows

There is a multitude of papers specially designed to make the business of wrapping presents colourful and exciting. People even make money gift wrapping parcels professionally these days, as a shop service. As well as the papers sold in most stationery stores, there are many other attractive papers which work well for wrapping.

Suitable wrappings

Wallpapers or varnished shelf papers are both suitable, although they need extra care when folding. To prevent the paper from cracking at the corners, plan the shape of the parcel and score a line with a knife on the outside of the paper where you want to fold it. Do this lightly, just breaking the outer fibres.

Tissue paper is pretty but fragile and needs special care. Because it is so thin, a gift usually needs more than one sheet to disguise the contents, and this gives the paper added strength and makes it easier to work with. You can achieve attractive effects by building up colours with several sheets and by overlapping or pleating them.

Crêpe paper has the advantage of stretching, so you can pull it to fit the shape of the parcel very neatly. It comes in a vast range of colours and is also available in a double-sided quality, with a different shade on each side.

Wrapping papers Even plain brown or white wrapping paper can look spectacular with contrasting ribbons or seals. Cellophane on top of any sort of paper gives a shiny glamour.

Posting parcels

When sending parcels by post, dispense with decorative ties and fancy ribbons and concentrate on making your parcel secure. Follow the same basic procedure as below but use stout brown paper and finish with plenty of string.

Rectangular boxes

Centre the paper under the box and wrap it round the box. Trim the overlap so that it can be turned under slightly (fig. 1). Trim the paper so that it extends over both ends of the box by a little more than half the depth of the box. Turn the overlap under and secure with concealed transparent sticky [cellophane] tape, either double-sided or folded double. Fasten the ends by folding in the sides, then turn the top flap down and the bottom flap up (fig. 2). Secure with concealed tape (fig. 3).

There are a variety of ways to use commercial gift ribbon—the kind that can be moistened and pressed together.

For posting [mailing]   To decorate parcels so that they can be over-wrapped with brown paper, bind with flat bands.

Simple bow   Fold over ends of a piece of ribbon and glue. Wrap a short piece round centre, and glue (fig. 4).

Tailored bow   Build up loops alternately to right and left. finishing with a small loop in the centre (fig. 5).

Knotless bow   Cut eight or more strips or ribbon 28cm (11in) long. Fold each piece separately, and assemble as shown (fig. 6).

Star bow   Make four larger and four smaller loops, assemble as shown and finish with one centre loop (fig. 7).

1. *Trim the overlap so that it can be turned under slightly.*
2. *Fasten the ends by turning the top flap down and the bottom flap up.*
3. *Secure with concealed tape.*
4. *Simple bow.*
5. *Tailored bow.*
6. *Knotless bow.*
7. *Star bow.*

Making decorative bows

Spaghetti bow   For a 12.5cm (5in) bow cut a 1cm ($\frac{3}{8}$in) wide piece of ribbon into 14 pieces each 40cm (16in) long. Make a figure '8' from each piece. Moisten or glue and secure at the centre (fig. 8). Moisten or glue and attach one figure '8' crosswise at the centre of another (fig. 9). Continue attaching figure '8's until bow is complete (fig. 10).

Swirl bow   Criss-cross four pieces of 28cm (11in) gift ribbon and stick together (fig. 11). Join the ends of each piece of ribbon to form a ball shape (fig. 12). Moisten the inside centre of the criss-cross. Twist the top a quarter turn and press firmly to the bottom (fig. 13).

Butterfly bow   Pinch six ribbon circles into oval shapes (fig. 14). Moisten and attach the six ovals at one end to form wings. Make up three others. Cut body from black ribbon (fig. 15) Cut a strip of ribbon approximately 15cm (6in) long for antennae. Fold in centre and form rings at both ends (fig. 16). Attach wings and antennae to body of butterfly (fig. 17).

Sunburst bow   Make a knotless bow. (See earlier instructions.) With sharp scissors, snip two slashes (from opposite directions) into the outer edge of each loop (fig. 18).

8-10. Spaghetti bow
11-14. Butterfly bow
15-17. Swirl bow
18. Sunburst bow.

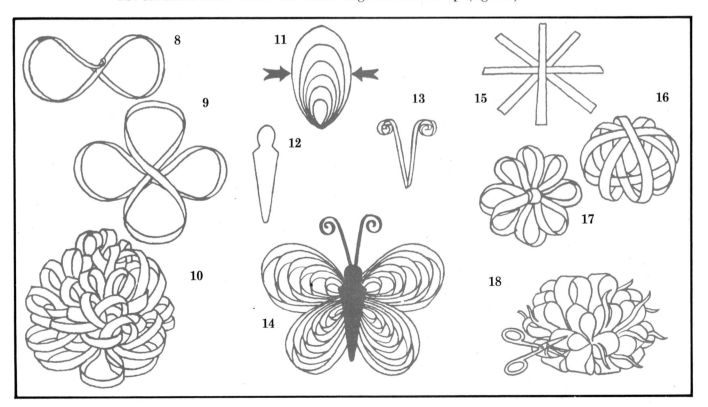

128

Small ribbon and tissue flowers

Tissue roses
1. Fold in half lengthways.
2. Roll and bunch up the tissue.
3. Cut leaves from a square of green tissue.

A cluster of enchanting small flowers, made from strips of tissue, crepe paper or self-stick ribbon, turns any gift parcel into a more personal and original gift. You could also make some to stand in a small pot on a table for festive occasions; sew some on to velvet for a pretty headband or attach them to hairpins stuck in a polystyrene ball on a length of dowelling to make a tiny ornamental tree. Stand it in a small plastic pot and set in a cellulose filler or fill the pot with pebbles to make it stand firmly.

Tissue roses

You will need:
1 sheet of red, pink or yellow tissue paper. (Each sheet will make about 16 small roses.)
1 sheet of green tissue paper.
Paste.

Ribbon roses

You will need:
2.5 (1in) wide self-stick gift-wrap ribbon in colours of your choice and green for leaves.

Ribbon poinsettia

You will need:
2.5cm (1in) wide self-stick, gift-wrap ribbon in red or yellow.

Tissue roses

For a rose 4cm (1½in) high, cut a piece of tissue 9cm (3½in) wide and 25cm (10in) long. Fuller roses can be 9cm (3½in) wide and 51 cm (20in) long.

the rose is formed. Roll the centre tightly; vary the squeezes and folds by bunching more in some places than others. Secure with paste. Cut a 5cm (2in) square of green tissue for leaves and cut into shape (fig.3). Roll round the bottom of the rose and stick in place or tie with matching sewing thread.

Ribbon roses

Cut a 51cm (20in) strip of ribbon. Holding it in the left hand, 2.5cm (1in) from the end, roll the ribbon inwards to form a tight core—approximately six turns (fig. 4). Fold the ribbon at a right angle towards the core, forming a diagonal edge (fig. 5). Crease the fold from A to B. Rotate the core, keeping points A and B level with the top of the core (fig. 6). At the end of each crease, fold again at a right angle, crease again and rotate core (fig. 7). Repeat until the rose is the desired size. Moisten the end and wrap round the core to fasten (fig. 8). Cut some leaves from green ribbon (fig. 9). Moisten and wrap round the base for a stem.

Ribbon poinsettia

Cut three strips of ribbon in each of these lengths; 15.5cm (6in),

12.5cm (5in), and 10cm (4in). Cut both ends of each piece to a sharp point (fig. 10). Moisten the centres and twist the centre of each strip to form two petals (fig.11). Moisten the centres of the medium-size petals and join them together. Repeat with the larger and smaller petals (fig. 12). Moisten the centres of the medium-size petals and join them to the largest petals. Add the smallest petals. Add a circle of coloured ribbon to the centre (fig.13).

Ribbon roses
4. *Roll strip of ribbon inwards.*
5. *Fold the ribbon at a right angle towards the core.*
6. *Rotate the core.*
7. *At end of each crease, fold crease again and rotate core.*
8. *Wrap around core to fasten.*
9. *Cut out leaves.*

Ribbon poinsettia
10. *Cut ends of each strip to a sharp point.*
11. *Twist to form two petals.*
12. *Repeat with other petals.*
13. *Add a circle of coloured ribbon to the centre.*

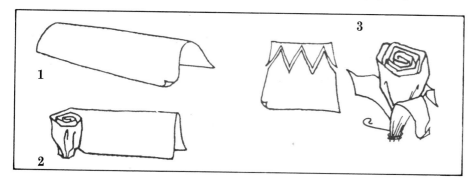

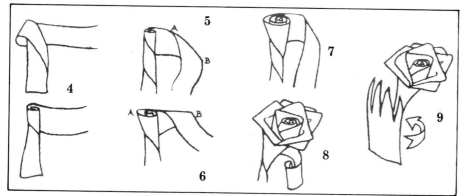

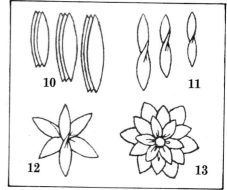

Glossary of papers

Artist's paper   See Cartridge paper.

Bristol board   This is a good quality board made from fine rag paper pressed together. It comes in a range of weights and will take paint very well.

Cardboard   An inexpensive board available in many colours. It will not crease or fold successfully and can really only be used flat. If it has a smooth surface it is suitable for poster colours, inks, model making and abstract ornaments.

Cartridge paper [Heavy bond paper/Artist's paper]   Basically a printing paper, but used extensively as a drawing paper. It comes in a variety of thicknesses and the colour ranges from white to pale buff. It is suitable for water-colour, ink sketching, charcoal, pencil and colour tinting, brass rubbing, pattern making and paper sculpture.

Cast coated paper and board   This is the highest grade of coated paper or board with a very smooth shiny surface which takes paint very well. The board is used for boxes and greetings cards. The paper has the same qualities but is finer.

Cover boards and papers Paper weight starts at around 110-120 grams per square metre and extends through board weight to about 500 grams per square metre. Both paper and boards come in a wide range of colours and finishes. The antique finish is available in embossed finishes – some subtle such as sand grained and some pronounced such as fabric or leather. This kind of paper folds and creases well without cracking. [Cover boards and papers are relatively unknown in North America. **Heavy construction paper** may be suitable for some projects.]

Crêpe paper   A form of tissue paper. The crinkled effect is achieved by passing the paper through a patterned roller while still wet. It comes in a wide range of colours and is easily malleable but will stretch. This can be an advantage, in that it can be moulded—or a disadvantage because once it is stretched, it will never shrink back. Double crêpe paper, which consists of two sheets of crêpe paper bonded together, is particularly useful for flower making.

Detail paper This is a translucent paper, cheaper and less stable than tracing paper. It is not very malleable and tends to crack. It is used in drawing offices for transferring designs.

Drawing papers and boards These are made from pure rag fibres, and are particularly suitable for water-based paints. The boards have the same qualities as the paper but are more rigid, so that the finished picture is self mounted.

Duplex paper Quite a stiff paper with a different colour on each side. It is made by rolling together two sheets of different colours while still wet, or coating one sheet with a different colour on each side. It is not always easily available.

Embossed paper This is made by running paper through rollers which are engraved with a design. The harder the paper, the more apparent the pattern. They are available in a wide variety of designs and qualities, and can be used for textures in such things as collage.

Fluorescent coated paper and board This is easily foldable and generally used for decorations.

Foil paper This is coated with adhesive, dusted with powdered metals and then burnished to produce a metallic finish. Embossed foil papers are also available.

Hand-made papers These are expensive and only available in a few shops. They have an interesting, non-mechanical appearance. Since any vegetable texture can be incorporated into the paper there is great scope for making different types of paper.

Heavy bond paper See Cartridge paper.

Ingres paper This tends to be expensive. It has an unusual and non-mechanical appearance with hair-like fibres showing on the surface of the sheet—this texture may be used in craft work. This paper folds well and does not crack.

Ivory board Hard white boards made by pasting two or more webs of paper together. It has a beautiful finish and is expensive. Very thin white cardboard is a cheaper substitute for beginners.

Japanese papers These are hand-made from exceptionally long fibres to produce either fine or white vellum papers which are very tough because the fibres pull apart rather than tear.

Kraft paper The word *kraft* means strength. Kraft paper is primarily designed for wrappings and carriers, but has many other applications. It is strong and foldable, and comes in white and a variety of colours. The white paper comes in a bleached form for a cleaner look, or unbleached in which case you tend to see bits and pieces in the surface.

Laid papers When a laid paper is made, the mould consists of wires laid side by side which make an impression on the paper. Paper that is made on a woven wire mould and has no such lines is called wove paper.

Manilla is strong flexible paper made from manilla hemp. It does not bleach easily and always comes in a brown or off white.

Marbled paper and board Marbling is a finish which can be done on machine or hand-made paper. It is mainly used for end-papers in book-binding. Marbling can be done on all types and qualities of paper and board.

Metallized paper and boards These come in a variety of weights and can be printed with metallic inks or laminated with foil. Available in gold, silver or colours—bright or matt. They are malleable, but tend to crease.

Poster paper Usually available from art shops, poster paper is coloured on one side only with a gloss or matt finish. Suitable for painting, origami and background colour work.

Pulp boards These are at the bottom end of the board market (ivory board is at the top). They come in a range of thicknesses and colours and have a smooth surface. They are more difficult to fold than cover boards because the crease tends not to follow a clean line. It is helpful to smooth the crease into place with a blunt knife.

Release papers are silicon-coated papers that will not take colour. They are used domestically for keeping sticky things apart. A circle of release paper placed on top of paint in a tin before replacing the lid will prevent a skin forming on the paint.

Self-adhesive paper is designed for labels but can be bought in sheets of small sizes and many colours. Some are backed with a permanent adhesive—others have non-permanent adhesive which may be more useful because when it gets tatty you can peel it off.

Stencil paper   This is stiff paper which has been specially treated to withstand repeated applications of paint. It is quite expensive and is possible to improvise by sealing ordinary cardboard with varnish.

Strawboards   This is the cheapest type of board available. The straw from which they are made is clearly visible on the surface but it can be laminated.

Tissue paper   This is a soft delicate paper available in a wide range of colours—glazed or matt. It creases but can be ironed smooth. The colours tend to fade in bright light and if it gets wet, the colours may run. It is suitable for various paper crafts.

Tracing paper   This is better quality than detail paper and more expensive. It has translucent qualities and is specially designed so that an erasure does not leave a mark.

Vellum paper is a natural cream colour rather than white. It has a smooth, good surface for writing on with ink. It is usually wove although laid vellum paper is also available.

Wallpapers   Some wallpapers do not stretch and can be rehung, others not. PVC [vinyl] wallpaper is wallpaper with a PVC [vinyl] coating.

Wove paper See Laid papers

Writing papers   These are primarily designed for writing but can be used for other purposes. The most expensive are the hand made papers—regrettably almost non-existent now. Then come the machine-made rag papers which are tub sized, that is, the paper is totally immersed in a tub of size which gives it better printing potential. A cheaper variety are the all rag or high rag content papers which are air dried, that is, dried by a special process which means that the paper will not gain or lose moisture from the atmosphere and, therefore, will not shrink or expand. Marbled paper is available in both laid and wove, and will take virtually any ink. Cheaper still are the high quality bonds.

Index

Pictures supplied by
Steve Bicknell p.32, 78
Camera Press p.39, 40, 53, 102T
Cent Idees de Marie Claire 24 & 25 (Boys);
22 (Godeaut)
Ray Duns p.29, 47
Geoffrey Frosh p.60, 61, 63, 64, 124R
Melvin Grey p.1, 35, 46, 59, 66, 68
Paul Kemp p. 105, 122
David Levin p.95, 96
Chris Lewis p.10B, 11R, 13, 15L, 16R
Maison de Marie Clare/Korniloff p.98
Dick Millar p.5, 18, 19, 36, 41, 42, 44, 45, 77, 131
Keith Morris p.129
Alasdair Ogilvie p.37, 49, 81, 91B
Tony Page p.65
Roger Phillips p.88, 90B
Kim Sayer p.102B, 103, 110
Jerry Tubby p.9, 27, 52, 125
Liz Whiting p.86, 92, 99

Artwork
Joanna Baii p.7, 9R, 10T, 11L, 13, 14, 15R, 16L
Marilyn Day p.79, 80
Victoria Drew p.82, 83, 85, 87, 91C
Dover Publications Inc., New York p.26CL,
  BL
Terry Evans p.127
Barbara Firth p.30, 31, 35R, 67, 70, 71, 73, 74,
  76, 77R, 117, 118, 119, 121
Trevor Lawrence p.18B, 20, 26,BR 123,
  124L
Coral Mula 100, 101
Mike Rose p.10, 11, 26
Gary Shewring p.54, 55
Kate Simunek p.128
Paul Williams p.89, 90T, 91T, 107, 108, 109,
111, 112, 113, 114